Rhinegold Study Guides

A Student's Guide to GCSE Music

for the **OCR** Specification
2005 onwards

by

David Bowman, Michael Burnett,
Ian Burton and Paul Terry

Rhinegold Publishing Ltd
241 Shaftesbury Avenue
London WC2H 8TF
Telephone: 020 7333 1720
Fax: 020 7333 1765
www.rhinegold.co.uk

Rhinegold Music Study Guides
(series editor: Paul Terry)

A Student's Guide to GCSE Music for the OCR Specification
Listening Tests for Students (Books 1 and 2): OCR GCSE Music Specification

A Student's Guide to AS Music for the OCR Specification
A Student's Guide to A2 Music for the OCR Specification
Listening Tests for Students: OCR AS Specification
Listening Tests for Students: OCR A2 Specification

Similar books have been produced for the AQA and Edexcel Music Specifications. Also available are:
A Student's Guide to GCSE Music for the WJEC Specification (separate English and Welsh language versions)
A Student's Guide to Music Technology for the Edexcel AS and A2 Specification
Listening Tests for Students: Edexcel AS and A2 Music Technology Specification

The following books are designed to support all GCSE and A-level music courses:
A Student's Guide to Composing (Book 1 for GCSE and Book 2 for A-level Music)
A Student's Guide to Harmony and Counterpoint (for AS and A2 Music)

Other Rhinegold Study Guides
Students' Guide to AS Classical Civilisation for the AQA Specification
Students' Guides to AS and A2 Drama and Theatre Studies for the AQA and Edexcel Specifications
Students' Guides to AS and A2 Performance Studies for the OCR Specification
Students' Guides to AS and A2 Religious Studies for the AQA, Edexcel and OCR Specifications

Rhinegold Publishing also publishes Classical Music, Classroom Music, Early Music Today, Music Teacher, Opera Now, Piano, Teaching Drama, The Singer, British and International Music Yearbook, British Performing Arts Yearbook, Music Education Yearbook, Rhinegold Dictionary of Music in Sound.

First published 2002 in Great Britain by
Rhinegold Publishing Ltd
241 Shaftesbury Avenue
London WC2H 8TF
Telephone: 020 7333 1720
Fax: 020 7333 1765
www.rhinegold.co.uk
Reprinted 2003, 2004, 2006
© Rhinegold Publishing Ltd

All rights reserved. No part of this publication may be reproduced, stored in a retrieval system, or transmitted in any form or by any means, electronic, mechanical, photocopying, recording or otherwise, without the prior permission of Rhinegold Publishing Ltd.
This title is excluded from any licence issued by the Copyright Licensing Agency, or other Reproduction Rights Organisation.
Rhinegold Publishing Ltd has used its best efforts in preparing this guide.
It does not assume, and hereby disclaims, any liability to any party
for loss or damage caused by errors or omissions in the Guide
whether such errors or omissions result from negligence, accident or other cause.

You should always check the current requirements of the examination, since these may change.
Copies of the OCR Specification may be obtained from Oxford, Cambridge and RSA Examinations at
OCR publications, PO Box 5050, Annesley, Nottingham, NG15 0DL
Telephone 0870 770 6622, Fax 0870 770 6621
See also the OCR website at www.ocr.org.uk

A Student's Guide to GCSE Music for the OCR specification
British Library Cataloguing in Publication Data.
A catalogue record for this book is available from the British Library.
ISBN 1-904226-02-7
Printed in Great Britain by WPG Group Ltd

Contents

Introduction . . . . page 5

Understanding Music 6

Performing 18

Composing 24

Terminal Task 37

Areas of Study:

      Exploiting the Resource. 41

      Techniques of Melodic Composition. 56

      Dance Music 73

      Traditions and Innovation 86

Glossary. 105

The authors

David Bowman was director of music at Ampleforth College for 20 years and was a chief examiner for the University of London Schools Examination Board (now Edexcel) from 1982 to 1998. David's publications include the *London Anthology of Music* (University of London Schools Examination Board, 1986), *Sound Matters* (co-authored with Bruce Cole, Schott, 1989), *Aural Matters* (co-authored with Paul Terry, Schott, 1993), *Aural Matters in Practice* (co-authored with Paul Terry, Schott, 1994), *Analysis Matters* (Rhinegold, Volume 1 1997, Volume 2 1998) and numerous analytical articles for *Music Teacher*. He is a contributor to the *Collins Music Encyclopedia* (2000), edited by Stanley Sadie, and author of the *Rhinegold Dictionary of Music in Sound* (2002).

Michael Burnett lectures in music at the University of Surrey, Roehampton where he has been involved in teacher training for almost 20 years. During that time Michael wrote and presented the BBC Schools radio programme *Music Box* for ten years. He was also seconded to the Jamaica School of Music for three years. Michael's compositions and arrangements have been widely published. He is the author of three books in the Oxford Topics in Music series for 11- to 14-year-olds, and arranger of several song and instrumental collections from IMP. He was series editor of the secondary-level teaching resource *Music File* (Stanley Thornes, 1991–1998), and regularly writes on music for the *Times Educational Supplement*.

Ian Burton is senior lecturer in music education at Huddersfield University. He previously ran the PGCE secondary-music course at Bath Spa University College, and was director of music for many years in comprehensive schools and colleges. He has been principal examiner in composing for OCR A-level music and a subject adviser for AQA GCSE music. He was involved with the development of the current A-level and GCSE music specifications and is a regular contributor to *Music Teacher*. He is a composer/arranger with particular interests in creating material for use in schools.

Paul Terry was director of music at the City of London Freemen's School for 15 years. He has been a music examiner for more than 20 years and has worked as a consultant to various examination boards. He was chief examiner for the Oxford and Cambridge Schools Examinations Board (now part of OCR) and for London Examinations (now part of Edexcel). Paul is co-author with William Lloyd of *Music in Sequence, a complete guide to MIDI sequencing* (1991), *Classics in Sequence* (1992) and *Rock in Sequence* (1996), and also *Rehearse, Direct and Play: A Student's Guide to Group Music-Making* (1993), all published by Musonix/ Music Sales.

Acknowledgements

The authors would like to thank Hallam Bannister, Lucy Green, Veronica Jamset, Lucien Jenkins, Elizabeth Ling, Robert Mason, Matthew Mellor, Graeme Rudland, Abigail Walmsley and Adrian York for their advice and support during the preparation of this guide. Nevertheless if any errors have been made it is only right to state that these are the responsibilities of the authors.

Warning. Photocopying any part of this book without permission is illegal.

Introduction

OCR's GCSE in Music is based on four areas of study:

1. Exploiting the Resource – knowing your instrument (or voice), including how to perform and how to compose for it
2. Techniques of Melodic Composition – how to study and write melodies
3. Dance Music – the Elizabethan pavan and galliard, the romantic waltz, disco from the 1970s and 1980s
4. Traditions and Innovation – salsa, bhangra, minimalism.

Your exam will be in three parts:

✦ **Coursework**

During the course you will have to give two performances (one solo and one ensemble) and produce two compositions. This coursework will be assessed by your teacher and the mark moderated by OCR. It is divided into two parts:

Part A (Integrated Coursework) is worth 35% of your total marks for the course. You will have to study at least three related pieces for your instrument (or voice) and perform one of them. You will also have to use ideas from this music as the basis for your own composition. Finally you will have to make an appraisal of your performance and your composition, showing how both relate to the pieces you have studied.

> In particular, you will have to employ your understanding of how your instrument is used in the pieces you have studied to help create your own composition.

Part B (Further Coursework) is worth a further 25% of your total marks. You will have to perform one piece and write a second composition. The composition must be related to Areas of Study 3 **or** 4.

✦ **Listening Paper**

This is a 75-minute paper marked by an OCR examiner and based on music from Areas of Study 2, 3 and 4. You will have to answer questions on a number of extracts of music played on CD. **These are unlikely to be the actual pieces that you have studied or that are discussed in this guide but they will be similar**. This paper is worth 25% of your total marks.

> We have included some examples of Listening Tests in this book, but you will get a much clearer idea of the requirements from *Listening Tests for Students Books 1 and 2: OCR GCSE Music Specification* (Rhinegold), for which a CD of recorded examples is also available.

✦ **Terminal Task**

This is a 30-minute paper based on Area of Study 2. You will be given an initial idea for a composition (called a stimulus) and you will have 30 minutes to create a performance based on this idea. There will be three ideas on the paper, from which you must choose the one you prefer: a rhythmic shape, a note pattern or a chord sequence. At the end of the exam you will have to present your completed melody in **one** of the following ways:

✦ By performing it
✦ By playing it with the help of ICT (eg a sequencer)
✦ By writing it down in music notation.

The Terminal Task is worth 15% of your total marks.

> **Warning.** Photocopying any part of this book without permission is illegal.

Understanding Music

This chapter covers some important terms and concepts that you will encounter during your course. Some of the points, particularly on keys and chords, may seem very difficult at first so don't try to work through the entire chapter in one go – use it as a reference source whenever you need to. Don't forget that the purpose of music theory is not to give you things to learn for homework but to help you become a better listener, performer and composer.

You will undoubtedly encounter many musical terms that are new to you. These will make much more sense if you understand the *sounds* to which they refer. Don't just rely on learning definitions, but play or sing the examples and use them in your own composing. Understanding musical terminology will help you convey to fellow musicians (even examiners!) complex ideas in just a word or two, rather than having to use long descriptions. But remember that musical terminology must be understood thoroughly and used correctly if it is to make sense.

To understand this chapter you will need to be able to read simple music notation. If you find this difficult try to spend some time early in the course getting yourself up to speed. There are many books on music notation and theory – your teacher will be able to suggest one that is appropriate. There are also websites and CD-Roms on the subject, and these often allow you to test yourself as you go. The best way of all though is to identify gaps in your knowledge and then ask your teacher for help. They won't mind – in fact they will be delighted if you are interested in improving your skills. And your teacher can explain things in the way you are most likely to understand if you find a concept hard to grasp. Remember that the best way to practise music-reading skills, and to explore new music, is to do as much sight-reading as you can manage.

Clefs

You will probably be familiar with the **treble clef**. Its symbol (𝄞) developed from an elaborate letter G which wraps around the line of the stave that represents the pitch G above middle C.

You will also encounter the **bass clef**. Its symbol (𝄢) developed from a letter F which wraps around the line of the stave that represents the pitch F below middle C.

The treble clef is used for melody instruments such as the flute, oboe, clarinet, saxophone, trumpet, horn, violin and recorder, as well as for treble and alto voices. The bass clef is used for bass voices and bass instruments such as the bassoon, trombone, tuba, cello and double bass. Keyboard instruments and the harp use both clefs.

The **vocal tenor clef** is easy to understand. It looks the same as a treble clef but with a small figure *8* at the bottom. This indicates that the music sounds an octave lower than the equivalent treble clef notes. It is used for tenor voices (hence its name) and for lead-guitar parts. Sometimes these parts are written in the normal treble clef, it being taken for granted that tenor singers and guitarists know that their part sounds an octave lower than written.

The symbol for the C clef (𝄡) developed from a letter C which wraps around the line of the stave that represents middle C. It can appear on the middle line of the stave, in which case it is known as the alto clef. Viola parts use this version of the C clef. It can also appear on the fourth line up of the stave, in which case it is known as the tenor clef. The tenor clef is used for the higher notes of the cello, double bass, bassoon and trombone. You will not need to become expert in reading the C clef unless you choose to use it in your compositions.

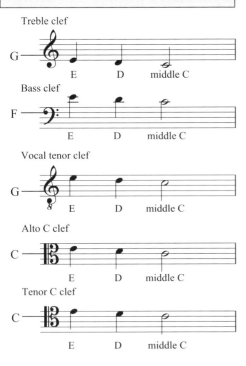

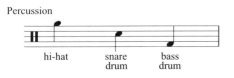

The examples *above left* show the first three notes of *Three Blind Mice* in all five of these clefs. Notice that all five end on middle C and they all sound exactly the same. The stave in the example *left* uses a percussion clef. It doesn't indicate pitches at all, but it enables a stave to be used for a variety of drum-kit sounds of indefinite pitch.

Major scales and major keys

Scales are one of the main building-blocks in many types of music. We may not enjoy playing them, but they are essential in building up an understanding of how music works.

An interval is the distance between two pitches. The smallest interval normally used in western music is a semitone. On the keyboard diagram *below* there is a semitone between notes 1 and 2, and another semitone between notes 2 and 3. The interval between notes 1 and 3 is therefore two semitones, or a tone.

'Semi' means 'half', so a semitone is half a tone.

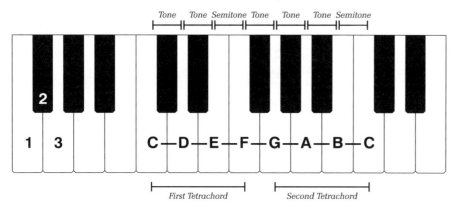

Now look at the scale of C major shown on this diagram. There is no black note between E and F, or between B and C. This is because these notes are already only a semitone apart.

Can you see the pattern of intervals in this scale? It starts with a group of four notes (known as a tetrachord) that are separated by the intervals tone–tone–semitone, and it ends with another group of four notes in exactly the same pattern. The last note of the first tetrachord and the first note of the second are a tone apart. So the entire eight-note scale makes the pattern:

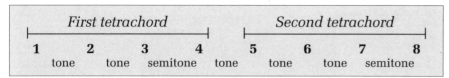

It may seem complicated but once you understand the pattern you can construct every major scale there is!

Let's put theory into practice and use the formula to construct a major scale starting on G. The first tetrachord will be G–A–B–C, which happens to be the same as the second tetrachord of C major (see *right*). We know that the other tetrachord must start a tone above the last note of the first tetrachord. To keep to the invariable tone–tone–semitone pattern it will have to consist of the notes D–E–F♯–G.

The important difference between the notes of C major and G major is that the former contains F♮ while the latter contains F♯. Keys which have most of their notes in common like this are described as being closely related.

Now try constructing a scale of D major. It begins with the second tetrachord of G major, shown left (D–E–F♯–G) and it ends with the tetrachord A–B–C♯–D. This scale is closely related to G major (only one pitch, C♯, is different) but less closely related to C major (where two pitches, F♯ and C♯, are different).

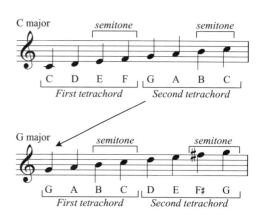

Warning. Photocopying any part of this book without permission is illegal.

Understanding Music 7

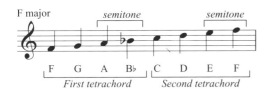

Follow the pattern one more time and write out a major scale starting on A. You should find that this time you need three sharps. Do you notice that every time you start a new scale on the fifth note of the previous scale, it needs one more sharp?

Now try writing out the major scale that starts on the fourth note of C major (F). In order to maintain our usual pattern you should end up with the scale of F major shown *left*. We can see that it is closely related to C major because both keys have all notes except one (B♭) in common. Repeat the process by starting a scale on the fourth note of F major (B♭), and you should find that the new scale needs two flats (B♭ and E♭). You have probably guessed by now – every time you start a new scale on the fourth note of the previous scale, it needs one more flat.

Rather than writing a sharp or flat before each note that needs one it is more convenient to use a key signature at the start of each stave to indicate the sharps or flats required, as shown *below*.

There are 12 possible major keys in all, and you can see their relationships in the following diagram. Keys next to each other in the circle are closely related. Notice that, at the top of the circle, the notes in the key of F♯ major (six sharps) sound the same as the notes in the key of G♭ major (six flats). They are said to be enharmonic equivalents, which means that they sound the same but are written differently.

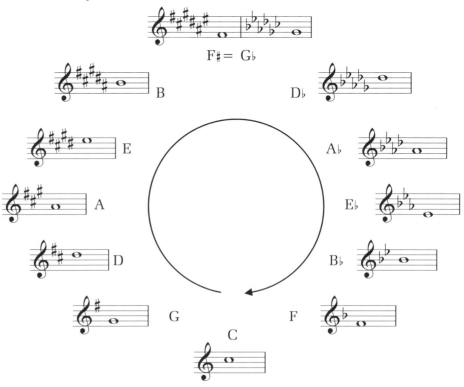

Notice that if you go round the circle clockwise from C major you add a sharp for each new key until you get to six sharps. It is then more sensible to use flats – and you must deduct a flat for each new key until you get back to C major.

When you write out a key signature the sharps or flats are always used in the fixed order shown above. If you need to use the bass clef, follow the order given in the example shown *left*.

8 Understanding Music

Scale degrees

It is often more convenient to refer not to individual note names but to the function of each note in a scale. For example the first note of a major (or minor) scale is always the key note, or tonic, whatever key the music is in. Here are the technical names for each degree of the scale – Roman numerals are often used instead of the technical names:

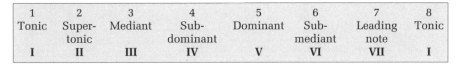

Earlier we saw how one of the most closely related keys to the tonic is the one a 5th higher than the tonic – so you won't be surprised to see that V is called the dominant. In the example below we can see that the dominant note of G is D. Similarly, the dominant key of G major is D major.

Test yourself on major scales and keys

1. Write out the scale of E♭ major in the treble clef. Which note is the dominant of E♭ major?

2. Write out the scale of A major in the bass clef. Which note is the subdominant of A major?

Minor scales and minor keys

Paired with every major key is a minor key with the same key signature. This **relative minor** is another key that is closely associated with the original tonic. It always starts on the submediant (sixth note) of its related major key. So the relative minor of C major starts on A and is called A minor. Instead of counting up six steps to find the starting note, you may prefer to think of it as two scale steps below the tonic:

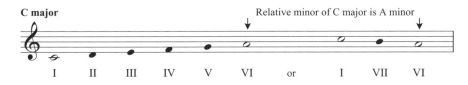

We can say that A minor is the relative minor of C major, or we can say that C major is the relative major of A minor. The starting note (or tonic) of all other minor keys is worked out in exactly the same way. So, what is the relative minor of each of the following keys: G major, D major, F major, B♭ major, A major, E♭ major?

Minor keys are sometimes misleadingly described as sad and major keys as happy. Fast music in a minor key can sound brilliant, stormy or angry, just as slow music in a major key can sound tragic or nostalgic. If asked to identify a key as being major or minor in a listening test you will need to listen very carefully to the relationship between notes and not rely on simplistic descriptions of this kind.

Warning. Photocopying any part of this book without permission is illegal.

Understanding Music 9

Minor scales come in several different versions. The easiest one to start with is what is known in pop and jazz as the natural minor. It uses exactly the same notes as its relative major, but because it starts on a different tonic, the intervals between the notes in the scale are different:

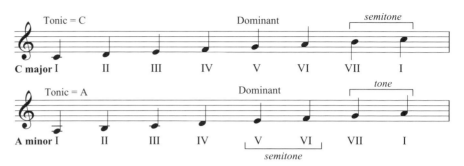

These differences are most obvious at the end of the scale. Play or sing several scales of C major, each time stopping on note VII. You will undoubtedly feel that the scale sounds incomplete unless the last note rises a semitone to finish on C, the tonic. This tendency is so strong that it gives note VII its technical name of leading-note – the note that needs to lead to the tonic.

The natural minor scale ends with an interval of a tone, and so doesn't display this tendency to the same extent. Repeat the experiment with the second example above, stopping on VII, and you will find that the need for it to rise to the tonic is less strongly felt.

The natural minor does not convey a strong sense of tonality (by which is meant a sense of key in which the tonic is the most important note). In order to establish a strong sense of key, the minor scale needs to end with the same rising semitone between VII and I that is found in major keys. The easy way to achieve this is to raise note VII by a semitone, but this then creates a rather odd-sounding interval between notes VI and VII:

If you have had to prepare scales for exams you may recognise that this example is a harmonic minor scale – it is better suited for harmonising music than for use in melodies because of the awkward interval between notes VI and VII.

To avoid this awkward interval, note VI is also often raised by a semitone, giving the following version of a minor scale:

You may recognise that this example comes from the melodic minor scale, which is better suited for melody writing. It has the pattern shown here when ascending, but it uses the natural-minor scale pattern when descending.

In a minor-key piece you may thus find notes VI and VII in both normal and raised versions:

10 Understanding Music

However the raised version of the leading note followed by the tonic (shown bracketed above) is needed to convey a firm sense of minor tonality, and the presence of this pattern is a clear indicator that the key is minor.

Notice that raising the pitch of notes VI and VII does not always mean using a sharp. If either of these notes is normally flat, then you will need a natural, not a sharp, to raise its pitch by a semitone:

Try to build up speed and accuracy in recognising keys, scales and the degrees of the scale – it will help you understand topics covered later on, particularly chords, very much more easily.

Test yourself on minor scales and keys

1. Name the relative minor of F major and state the pitch of its raised leading note. ....

2. Write out the scale of G minor in the treble clef, using the raised form of the sixth and seventh degrees of this scale.

3. Name the key of the following passage of music:......................

Vivaldi, Op.3 No.2

Other scales and modes

The **pentatonic scale** is a five-note scale found in folk music in many different parts of the world. The major pentatonic scale uses notes 1–2–3–5–6 of the major scale (see *right*). If you play a scale on just the black notes of a keyboard, starting on F♯, you will hear the major pentatonic scale in F♯. The minor pentatonic scale uses notes 1, 3, 4, 5 and 7 of the natural minor scale (see *right*).

Major pentatonic scale starting on C

Minor pentatonic scale starting on C

The pentatonic scale is very useful when you first start composing because, since it doesn't include any semitones, it is possible to combine melodic lines and use simple drone accompaniments without creating harsh dissonances.

Unlike the pentatonic scale, the **chromatic scale** consists entirely of semitones, 12 of them to the octave:

Chromatic scale

The **whole-tone scale** proceeds entirely in steps of a tone:

Understanding Music 11

Whole-tone scale

Aeolian mode

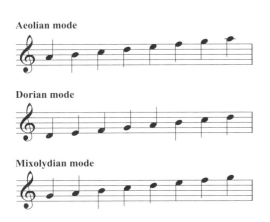

Dorian mode

Mixolydian mode

A **mode** is simply a set of notes. The major scale is one kind of mode and the natural minor scale that we saw on page 10 is another – indeed, it is the same as the aeolian mode printed *left*. This example shows three of the most common modes. The significant difference between major scales and modes is the relationship of the notes within the mode. Notice that none of those printed here ends with a semitone between its last two notes – one of the characteristic features of a major scale. For GCSE you will not be required to distinguish between the different types of mode, but you might be expected to recognise that a passage is modal rather than major or minor.

Intervals

Remember that an interval is the distance between two notes. If the two notes occur simultaneously they form a harmonic interval. If they occur in succession they form a melodic interval, either ascending or descending. All are described in the same way, by counting the letter names from the lower note to the higher note. Always count the lower note as 1. The intervals shown *left* are all 5ths.

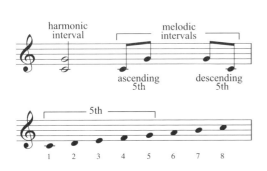

However, describing intervals by number alone is insufficient. For instance, the interval from D to F is a 3rd – but so is the interval from D to F# and they are clearly not the same. We need to add a description of the 'quality' of the interval in order to be more precise.

To do this, imagine that the lower note of the interval is the key note (or tonic) of a major scale. If the upper note belongs to that scale the interval will be named as follows:

(perfect) major major perfect perfect major major (perfect) major
unison 2nd 3rd 4th 5th 6th 7th octave 9th

In every major and minor scale, you'll find that the intervals between the tonic and fourth, fifth and octave are called 'perfect'.

If the interval is one semitone smaller than a major interval with the same two letter names, it is a minor interval. That gives us the following possibilities:

minor minor   minor minor   minor
2nd   3rd   6th   7th   9th

The minor 2nd sounds the same as a semitone and the major 2nd sounds the same as a tone. Notice how you have to stagger the note heads when writing these small intervals on a single stave.

If an interval is one semitone smaller than a minor or perfect interval with the same two letter names, it is diminished. And if an interval is one semitone larger than a major or perfect interval with the same two letter names, it is augmented:

major minor diminished perfect diminished perfect augmented major augmented
7th   7th   7th   5th   5th   4th   4th   2nd   2nd

12 Understanding Music

The diminished 5th and the augmented 4th sound the same when heard in isolation. Both consist of an interval of three tones, and each is therefore often called a **tritone**.

Notice that you can alter the quality of an interval by changing either of its notes. The diminished 7th in the previous example is a semitone smaller than the minor 7th because its lower note has been raised by a semitone.

> **Naming intervals: a summary**
>
> First work out the number of the interval. Next decide if the upper note is in the major scale of which the lower note is the tonic. If it is, the interval will be major or perfect. If not, the following rules usually help:
>
> If the interval is a semitone smaller than a major interval with the same two letter names, it is minor.
>
> If the interval is a semitone smaller than a minor or perfect interval with the same two letter names, it is diminished.
>
> If the interval is a semitone larger than a major or perfect interval with the same two letter names, it is augmented.

One of the most confusing things about naming intervals is the fact that minor intervals occur in major keys, and major intervals occur in minor keys.

Let's see how this works in practice with the examples shown *right*. First work out the number of the interval, remembering to count the lower note as 1. Interval (a) is a 3rd (F=1, G=2, A=3). Next imagine the lower note (F) to be the tonic. Does the upper note (A) occur in the key of F major? Yes! So this is a major 3rd.

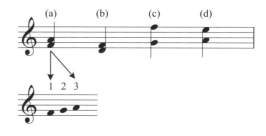

Example (b) is also a 3rd. Imagine the lower note (D) to be the tonic. Does the upper note (F) occur in the key of D major? No! The third note in D major is F♯, but here we have an F♮ – so interval (b) is a semitone less than a major 3rd. It is a minor 3rd.

Now work out interval (c). The lower note is G. Does the upper note (F) occur in G major? If it doesn't, this cannot be a major interval. What interval is it? Work out interval (d) for yourself.

Test yourself on intervals

Write the named harmonic interval by adding a note *above* each of the following notes.

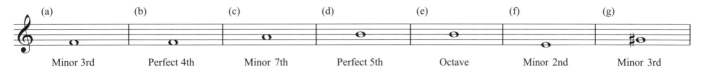

Triads

The simplest type of chord is the **triad**. It consists of three pitches: the note on which the chord is based (the **root**), along with a 3rd and 5th above it. Here are the triads on each note of a C-major scale:

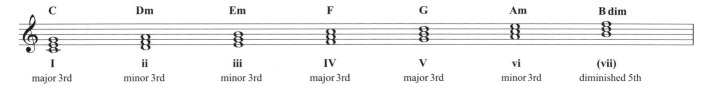

Upper-case Roman numerals (I, II, etc) are often used to indicate major triads while lower-case Roman numerals (i, ii, etc) can be used to indicate minor triads.

Triads can be described by using the technical names or the Roman numerals that are used for naming the degrees of the scale. For instance, in the key of C major the dominant chord (chord V) is simply the triad on the dominant note (G).

Look carefully at the interval between the root and third of each chord in the previous example. In chords I, IV and V the middle note is a major 3rd above the root. These are therefore major chords, and are known as the three primary triads. In chords ii, iii and vi the middle note is a minor 3rd above the root. These are known as minor chords.

The interval between the root and top note is a perfect 5th in every triad except vii. Here the outer interval is a diminished 5th and this triad is therefore known as a diminished triad.

In pop and jazz it is more usual to notate chords by writing the letter name of the root above the stave. A single capital letter indicates a major chord. A lower case 'm' after a capital letter indicates a minor chord, while 'dim' indicates a diminished triad.

The notes of a chord can be positioned in any octave, with any spacing and with notes duplicated. All of the chords shown *left* are G major – even the last one can be assumed to be G major, despite the fact that one of the notes (the 5th, D) is omitted.

Notice that the root of the triad (G) is the lowest note of all five chords in this example. When, as here, the root is the lowest note the chord is said to be in **root position**.

Inversions

If a chord is arranged so that the root is *not* the lowest note it is said to be inverted. If the 3rd is in the bass the triad is said to be in first inversion. This is indicated by adding the letter 'b' to the appropriate Roman numeral (see *left*: a root-position triad should have the letter 'a' after the Roman numeral, but it is usually omitted). You may also see a first inversion expressed as $^6_3$, indicating that the upper two notes are a 6th and a 3rd above the bass.

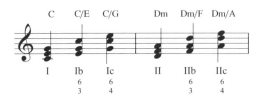

If the 5th is in the bass the triad is said to be in second inversion and this is indicated by adding the letter 'c' to the appropriate Roman numeral. You may see a second inversion expressed as $^6_4$, indicating that the upper notes are a 6th and a 4th above the bass.

It should now be clear that however the upper notes of a chord are arranged, the bass note is especially important. This is also true if you use chord symbols other than Roman numerals. If the bass note is not the root, write an oblique stroke after the chord symbol and then name the bass note required: e.g C/E indicates a chord of C major with E in the bass (in other words, a first inversion).

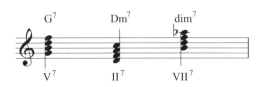

More elaborate chords can be formed by adding a 7th above the root – you will often see chords V and II embellished in this way, as shown *left*. If you add a diminished 7th to chord VII you will form a dramatic chord known as a diminished seventh.

It is also possible to add other notes to triads (such as 2nds or 9ths) and to make chromatic alterations to one or more of the notes of the triad. However while such techniques are well worth exploring when composing, they are beyond the requirements of GCSE.

Warning. Photocopying any part of this book without permission is illegal.

14 Understanding Music

Melodic decoration

If melodies only used notes from the current chord they would sound very dull, so basic harmony notes are frequently enlivened with various types of melodic decoration. These often create a momentary dissonance (a clash) with the underlying harmony.

These decorative (or unessential) notes may be **diatonic**, which means they use notes from the prevailing key, or they may be **chromatic**, meaning that they use notes from outside the prevailing key. And, although we have called this section melodic decoration, these embellishments may occur in the melody, bass or an inner part.

An **auxiliary note** lies a tone or a semitone above or below a harmony note and returns to it. A **passing note** moves by step between two harmony notes that are a 3rd apart. Passing notes normally occur on weak beats. If they occur on strong beats they will be much more obviously dissonant and are then known as accented passing notes.

An **appoggiatura** is a dissonance that is approached by a leap. The tension created is released when the appoggiatura 'resolves' by moving to a harmony note.

A **suspension** starts with a consonant note which is then sustained or repeated (ie suspended) over a change of harmony, causing a discord. The discord then resolves to a harmony note, usually by moving downwards by step. In most cases the suspension actually replaces one of the harmony notes. For instance in the example *right*, the normal 3rd of a C-major chord (E) has been temporarily replaced by F, a 4th above C. In pop and jazz, suspensions are often treated as chords in their own right and are notated with a separate chord symbol (C$^{sus\,4}$ in this case).

Figuration

If chords were always used as plain blocks of notes music would sound very boring. Even in a simple accompanied melody composers often make the accompaniment more interesting by devising patterns from chord notes. These patterns are known as figures, and can be adapted to fit changes in the chords. The example *right* shows just five ways of devising a figure from a C-major chord. Pattern (a) is a simple arpeggio figure, while (b) is a broken-chord figure known as an Alberti bass (named after a composer who over-used this type of figuration). The syncopation in pattern (c) gives this figure a more urgent feel. Patterns (d) and (e) both include unessential notes.

Motifs, phrases and cadences

A **motif** is a short melodic or rhythmic idea that is distinctive enough to maintain its identity despite being changed in various ways. It is often the basic cell from which much longer musical ideas are constructed, as in this example by Mozart:

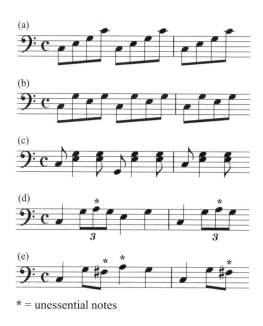

* = unessential notes

The opening motif (*x*) features a rhythm (♫|♩) and a falling

Understanding Music 15

semitone. First it is repeated exactly, then it is repeated and extended by an upward leap and a rest. Next it is adapted so that there is a fall to the third note (x^1). This variant is then treated in **sequence** (which means the *immediate* repetition of an idea at a different pitch). The last appearance is again extended to match the rhythm (but not the rising leap) of the first extension. In Mozart's Symphony No 41 the entire **phrase** quoted above is then repeated in sequence a step lower, creating a perfectly balanced pair of phrases.

The phrase above begins on the last beat of a bar. An opening on a weak beat like this is known as an **anacrusis**. It means that the music starts with an incomplete bar and the final bar of the phrase is shortened to balance. The example thus contains 16 beats in all and we can still refer to it as being a four-bar phrase, even though it doesn't fit into four complete bars. Notice how bars are numbered when there is an anacrusic start – bar 1 is the first *complete* bar.

Phrases often end with a **cadence** – a point of repose, rather like punctuation in a sentence. The perfect cadence (chords V–I) gives a sense of completion, rather like a full stop at the end of a sentence. The imperfect cadence (an ending on chord V) sounds open and incomplete – more like a comma after a phrase in a sentence:

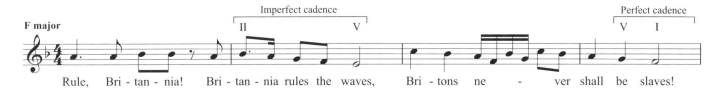

Note that chord V in an imperfect cadence can be preceded by any suitable chord (I, II or IV are the most usual).

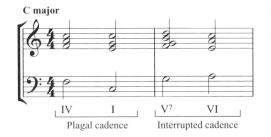

Two other cadences you may encounter are illustrated *left*. The plagal cadence consists of chords IV–I and is often associated with a sung 'Amen' in church music. The interrupted cadence begins with chord V (or V^7) like a perfect cadence, but it ends with almost any chord other than I – in other words, the expected perfect cadence is interrupted by an unexpected chord.

Modulation

The perfect cadence, particularly in the form V^7–I, has an important role in defining the key. Chord V^7 includes the leading note, which tends to want to rise to the tonic in chord I, while the seventh of chord V^7 tends to want to fall to the third in chord I. Look at the melody shown *left*, which clearly outlines a perfect cadence. The chord of C^7 includes B♭, so the key must be a flat key, but it also includes E♮. There are only two keys with this combination, F major and F minor. And when the 7th (B♭) drops to A♮ in the tonic chord we know that the key cannot be F minor – it can only be F major.

When you see accidentals in a passage of music, they can have any of the following functions:

Warning. Photocopying any part of this book without permission is illegal.

16   Understanding Music

- They may be the sixth and/or seventh degrees of a minor scale
- They may indicate that the music has modulated (changed key)
- They may be chromatic notes which have no effect on the key.

The role of the perfect cadence in defining key will enable us to differentiate between these different functions of accidentals. Look at the following melody by Sousa:

When you see an accidental, ask yourself if it might be a leading note – if it is, the tonic will be a semitone higher and you would expect to see a perfect cadence in this key. So, the presence of G♯ might suggest the key of A minor, and F♯ might suggest G minor. But there are no perfect cadences in either of these keys.

There are only two different chords, C⁷ and F, and these make a clear perfect cadence in F major in bars 5–8. The music is therefore in the key of F major, and G♯ and F♯ are both chromatic notes.

Next look at this simplified version of a minuet by Mozart. It also starts in F major, as confirmed by the perfect cadence (C⁷–F) in bars 3–4. The first accidental is B♮ in bar 5. Is this merely chromatic or does it signify a modulation? As always, test to see if it is a leading note (eg of C major) by looking for a perfect cadence in this new key. This time there are perfect cadences in the new key, in bars 5–6 (G⁷–C) and again in bars 7–8 (G–C). So B♮ is not a chromatic note – the music does indeed modulate to the key of C major.

Remember, for a modulation to take place you should expect to see not only accidentals that reflect the new key, but also a perfect cadence in the new key.

Understanding Music 17

Performing

Any instrument is allowed, including the voice, so when we refer to 'instrument' in this chapter we include singing.

During the course you will have to perform three pieces:

+ A solo (with or without accompaniment)
+ An ensemble in which you take a significant individual part
+ **Either** another solo **or** another ensemble piece.

The performances can be given at any time during the course, although all work must be submitted by the date published by OCR which is normally 15 May in your exam year. Your GCSE teacher will usually need to be present at your performances, which must all be recorded. You are allowed to repeat the pieces on different occasions if you are not satisfied, and then pick your best work for the exam.

Planning

Careful planning is essential. Your teacher will help you with this, but in general it is best to aim to complete all the coursework performing by about halfway through your final year. When you plan your schedule remember the following points:

+ You may need much more practice time than you expect, or you may have to substitute a different piece if something you have chosen proves to be too difficult
+ Illness or other commitments may mean that performances have to be postponed
+ Accompanists or other members of an ensemble may not be available for rehearsals when you expect
+ You may be dissatisfied with your performance and wish to repeat it a few weeks later
+ The recording of your performances may be lost or erased
+ You will probably be too busy with revision and completing other coursework to devote time to practising and performing in the final weeks before the exam.

This is a fearsome list but if any of these delays occurs it may take several weeks before you can find another performing opportunity, so it really is vital to plan ahead and not leave things until the end of the course.

It is likely that you will be able to give your performances during lesson time. It will certainly make it easier to arrange ensemble rehearsals and performances if you can form a group with other members of your GCSE music class.

Many students enjoy performing, but some find that it makes them very nervous. A few nerves are natural, but if you get very anxious try to find opportunities to perform as frequently as possible. Regular class concerts can help – start with a simple piece that you know well. As you gain confidence you will begin to become more relaxed and your playing or singing will improve as a result.

Warning. Photocopying any part of this book without permission is illegal.

Performance 1

As part of your coursework you will need to study at least three related pieces for your instrument, and perform one of them. These could be works that:

- Are in the same **genre** (such as a group of marches, perhaps from different periods of music history)
- Use the same form (such as a group of works in theme-and-variations form)
- Are in the same style (such as a group of baroque works or a group of blues songs)
- Use the same resources (such as a group of works for brass quartet).

This will need careful planning early in the course. You will need to decide what type of music you wish to focus on and then draw up a list of possible pieces. Your teacher(s) can help you with this. It would be a good idea to start with a list of six or more works. Then check the availability of any sheet music and recordings that you need before making your final selection.

One possible strategy is to include:

- The piece that you hope to perform
- An easier piece in case your first choice proves too difficult
- A more difficult piece that you don't intend to perform but that will teach you more about writing for your instrument
- Several additional pieces in case the ones above are not as useful as you first hoped.

The first of your compositions must relate to the works that you choose here (see page 25). For instance if you choose to study a group of works for jazz piano, your composition will need to demonstrate what you have learnt about jazz-piano styles.

It is worth spending some time working out the best strategy for this important part of the course. Initial plans may not always work out well and you may then have to start again with a different idea. This will not be a problem if you start planning early in the course.

If this seems complicated, remember that all of this work comes under the Area of Study called Exploiting the Resource (which we examine in detail on page 41). Essentially this is about how composers have written for your instrument, and what you can learn from their work in your own composing and performing. So choose your pieces with this in mind.

It is best to select works that show off your instrument to its best advantage. Very simple pieces often don't do this, which is why it is important to study (even if you don't perform) some more difficult music in your selection. Such pieces may give you more ideas for your own composition than simple pieces or arrangements.

After you have presented and recorded your piece you will have to give an appraisal of your performance showing how far you have realised the composer's intentions (see page 22).

Specification change
Those taking the exam in June 2007 and later should note that Performance 3 has been withdrawn from the syllabus and that candidates only need to offer one further performance as part of the further coursework component (Performance 2), in addition to a piece performed as part of the integrated coursework component (Performance 1). Students should also note that between Performances 1 and 2 both a solo piece and an individual part from an ensemble should be presented.

Warning. Photocopying any part of this book without permission is illegal.

Performance 2

The requirements here are simpler. Basically you just need to perform one more piece. This could be another item from the list you prepared for Performance 1, but it doesn't have to be – it could be any work that you know you can perform well. You do not have to write an appraisal of this performance.

Remember that between your two pieces you must include a solo (with or without accompaniment) and an ensemble piece in which you perform a significant independent part.

You don't have to use the same instrument for both of your performances, but there are no marks for showing that you can play more than one instrument. It is therefore sensible to concentrate on reaching a good standard on your main instrument.

Solo performance

Pieces that are intended to be accompanied should be presented with accompaniment, otherwise much of the music will be missing. Remember to have plenty of rehearsals with your accompanist. You can use a pre-recorded backing if you wish, providing that your own part can be clearly distinguished and is not doubled throughout most of the piece.

Remember that all musicians play better if they have a short warm-up first – this is especially important for wind players and singers. If you are an instrumentalist playing with accompaniment, take your time over careful tuning before you start. Play long notes and check several different pitches across the range (including your starting note) before you begin the piece.

Ensemble performance

For exam purposes, an ensemble must include you and at least one other person playing live. You must take a significant individual part in the ensemble, so performing the same part as others in a choir or band would not be suitable. It is permissible for the ensemble to use some pre-recorded material, such as a backing track, providing that it doesn't double your own part in most of the piece. However pre-recorded material could limit your ability to respond to the essentially live nature of ensemble playing, so it is best avoided.

Organisation is very important in ensemble work. Members of the group need to be clear about rehearsal times and places, and must remember to bring their instruments and music. Rehearsals will be more fun and more productive if everyone understands the difference between practising and rehearsing:

✦ Practising is done by each individual, before the group meets for the first time

✦ Rehearsing is done by the group, after all of its members have learnt at least the basics of their own individual parts.

Rehearsals should not be a time when individual players practise their parts. If that happens the rest of the group will quickly become bored.

An accompanied solo can count as an ensemble, but the piece must allow you and your accompanist to interact in order to get a good mark. An accompaniment that is purely supportive and that merely follows your lead is unlikely to make this possible.

Warning. Photocopying any part of this book without permission is illegal.

Careful tuning is vital in ensemble performance. Wind players must warm up before tuning, but once this is done the rest of the group must remain silent while each player tunes their instrument. If there is a piano or other fixed-pitch instrument, tune to that. Otherwise, tuning notes should be given on the instrument with the clearest sound.

Remember to adopt a good playing posture and then sound a long note at a moderately loud volume in order to check pitch – a quick toot will not be enough. Wind players should ensure that they produce the note with proper breath support. Each player should tune individually, and string players will need time to check all of their strings. Rock bands will also need to check the balance of their instruments. It is not necessary for the band to rehearse at anything like the volume needed for an actual gig – mistakes are much easier to hear and correct at low sound levels. Players of all electric instruments should keep a note of their settings in order to save time at the next rehearsal.

Finally, before starting to rehearse the music itself, try playing a few very slow scales in unison, listening carefully to each other's intonation – this exercise will also help give any singers a chance to warm-up before they start.

Improving your marks

Each piece is initially marked out of 30 for musicality. For a mark of five or more your performance will need to be fluent, show technical control and communicate the intention of the music with some success. For a top mark your performance will need to be confident, fluent, technically controlled and musically expressive. In short, it will be a memorable interpretation of the work.

Ensemble performing is marked in a similar way, although the criteria also stress the importance of coordination and balance with the rest of the group.

For each piece, up to 15 marks are then added to reflect the technical difficulty of the part you played. A simple piece which uses a limited range of notes and/or rhythms, with easy movement between notes and in an easy key, may attract no more than one additional mark. If the piece uses a wider range of notes and/or rhythms, and is more demanding in terms of key, articulation, phrasing and gradations of dynamics, then it can attract two or three extra marks. For four or five extra marks the piece will need to be more complex, use an extended range and make intricate demands in terms of control of tempo, dynamics and phrasing.

This needs a word of caution. Clearly a few more marks are available if you can manage more difficult music with confidence. But the majority of the marks are awarded for musicality, and one of the most important criteria is the fluency of your performance. If you frequently hesitate or stumble over difficult passages, or even have to stop completely, the presentation will not be fluent, and you will score few marks for musicality. You are likely to get a better mark by playing a simple piece well than attempting a difficult one that you haven't fully mastered.

Warning. Photocopying any part of this book without permission is illegal.

Also remember that you can maximise your marks by writing a really good appraisal of your Performance 1. We will look at this topic next.

Performance appraisal

You have to present an appraisal of your Performance 1. This can be written down or spoken and recorded on tape. You may well find it easier to present your appraisal in written form unless you can speak fluently about musical performance.

There are three essential things to include:

- ◆ How your instrument is used in the performance
- ◆ Similarities and differences between the piece you perform and the other two pieces you have studied
- ◆ The quality of your performance, including what you think was effective and what you think could have been improved.

You must keep to the above points. If you say things like 'Mozart was born in 1756, visited Italy and wrote 17 piano sonatas' you can be certain that you have gone wrong!

Be clear about what you want your listeners to experience when they hear your performance. Is it an image of sunlight, the chill of winter, a feeling of grandeur or a sense that they are dancing? Is it the beauty of your tone, the elegant balance of your phrasing or the excitement of hearing brilliantly articulated fingerwork?

You will not get many marks if you just say 'I played well ... I was very pleased that nothing went wrong'. However good you think you are, there is almost certainly room for improvement and in this part of the exam you will be expected to show that you are developing an ability for self-criticism.

Here is an appraisal that ought to score a good mark because it clearly explains what has been learnt about performing and it identifies how the performance might have been improved.

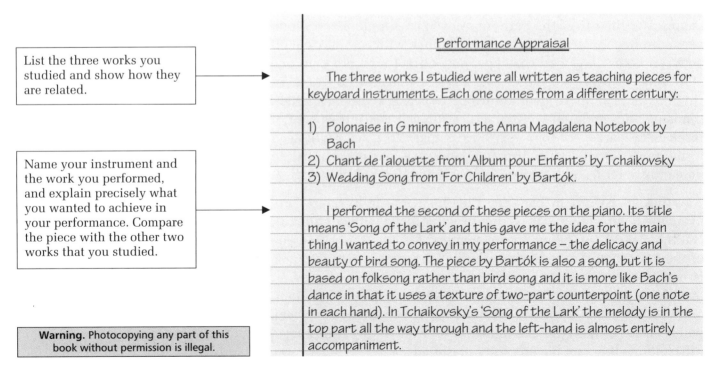

List the three works you studied and show how they are related.

Name your instrument and the work you performed, and explain precisely what you wanted to achieve in your performance. Compare the piece with the other two works that you studied.

Warning. Photocopying any part of this book without permission is illegal.

I played without using the sustaining pedal since there are no big stretches and the lack of pedal helped make the rapid triplets, staccato notes and ornaments much cleaner and more 'chirrupy' – more like a bird, in fact! I also play Bach's Polonaise without using the pedal. This is because it was written for the harpsichord or clavichord, which are instruments that do not have a sustaining pedal. When played on the piano the dance needs a crisp and delicate touch, just like Tchaikovsky's piece.

- The dynamics in Chant de l'alouette include many crescendos and diminuendos. It was sometimes difficult to make these changes as gradual as I wanted. The dynamics in Bach's Polonaise are quite different as they are either loud or quiet. Also they are only suggestions made by the modern editor and were not written by the composer.

There are no changes of speed marked in any of the three pieces, but in the Tchaikovsky I decided to make a big ritardando in bar 19 and then go back in tempo at bar 20, where the opening tune is repeated. I felt this was an effective way to lead into this final section and such changes of speed are typical of the romantic period in which this piece was written. It would not be a very stylish
- thing to do in music of other periods, though.

I had intended that the speed should be even throughout the rest of the piece, but unfortunately I had not learnt the final section too well and had to slow up in order to manage the very high notes. Luckily I was able to keep going, though, and didn't have to stop completely.

I was disappointed that the contrasts did not seem as effective as I had thought. The left hand sounded legato throughout – even the quaver chords that should have been separated – and some notes did not sound properly in places where I tried to play too quietly. The differences between loud and soft passages were also much less obvious than I had hoped.

I was pleased that I played most of the notes correctly, but I think I should have performed the piece with a wider range of expression and with better tone colour in the upper register of the piano.

> Explain how the resource (your instrument) is exploited in the piece you performed, and compare this with the other pieces you studied.

> Mention any aspects of the piece (such as tempo, articulation, dynamics or texture) that you felt were particularly effective – or that caused you particular problems – in your performance.

> Draw attention to aspects of your performance that you feel show a good awareness of style.

> Be honest about the things that went less well and say how they could be improved.

> Summarise the main points of your appraisal in a short final paragraph.

Warning. Photocopying any part of this book without permission is illegal.

Composing

When you begin your GCSE course you may find that composing a piece on your own is a new experience. Different people have different feelings about composing. Some may already have experimented with songs and chord patterns or may feel confident using a computer. Others may have a favourite composer or style of music they would like to study further. Many GCSE musicians see themselves mainly as performers and are rather daunted by the idea of composing. Wherever you are coming from, the GCSE course will provide you with starting points and composing techniques to help you find your own voice as a composer.

Requirements You will probably compose a number of pieces during your GCSE course, but you are required to submit just two compositions for assessment. Each of these should last no more than three minutes and both must be related to music that you explore in the Areas of Study as explained below.

Your teacher will tell you when your work needs to be ready – this is likely to be before 15 May in your examination year. It might be wise to aim to complete most of the work on your compositions by the start of the spring term of your examination year.

Composition 1 Composition 1 (integrated coursework) is based on Area of Study 1: Exploiting the Resource. You will need to:

- Compose a piece that features the instrument/voice that you use for the performing part of the exam
- Use in your composition musical features from pieces that you have studied and performed
- Make an appraisal of this composition.

Composition 2 Composition 2 (further composing) must be related to one of the core styles in Areas of Study 3 (Dance Music) or 4 (Traditions and Innovation). The core styles are:

- Pavan and galliard
- Waltz
- Disco music of the 1970s and 1980s
- Salsa
- Bhangra
- Minimalism.

Composing is also part of the Terminal Task (see page 37).

Starting points

For hundreds of years musicians have learned to compose by getting to know lots of music and finding out how other composers have constructed their pieces. They have then developed their own approaches in order to communicate something new. This is exactly what happens on your GCSE course. In the Areas of Study you will look at different types of music, discover techniques that composers have used and compose your own pieces using some of these techniques.

Don't think that composing using models is just something that happens at school. Bach learned his trade by copying out other composers' music. Elgar wrote a piece modelled on Mozart's 40th symphony. Mozart was still studying Bach's composing techniques towards the end of his life. All of these composers had strong musical styles of their own, and the techniques that they learned from other composers merged with their own styles. Immersing yourself in music is the best way to learn to compose.

> One good way to study music is to use MIDI files downloaded from the Internet. Just make sure if you use any material from the Internet in your own compositions that you acknowledge it, otherwise you could be accused of cheating.

Integrated coursework

Composition 1 (integrated coursework) forms part of the linked task in performing, composing and appraising that we introduced on page 19. There we explained how you must study three pieces, perform one of them and appraise your performance. You will also have to write a brief for your own composition. This brief needs to provide a blueprint for a piece that will let you show:

✦ That you understand the musical potential of your instrument or voice

✦ That you have identified and can use features drawn from the three pieces that you have studied.

Next you will compose a piece to meet your brief, and finally you will appraise your composition, considering:

✦ How well you have succeeded in fulfilling your original brief

✦ What features of the piece have been successful

✦ How successfully your piece relates to the three pieces that you studied.

> A brief is a set of instructions. Here it refers to a statement of what a composition is meant to achieve. Professional composers, especially those employed in the commercial world, often work to briefs. Being able to meet a brief is an essential part of the composer's job. If a TV producer asks for a three-minute salsa piece for five instruments and two voices then that is exactly what has to be provided. The producer knows the style needed for a particular programme, how long the time slot is and how many musicians they can afford to pay. If a composer is asked to write a three-minute fun piece for an amateur wind band to play, the musicians will not be impressed with a serious 15-minute piece that only has parts for half of the band members.

Although this process seems complicated it gives you lots of starting points for composing. Your performance and composition will be assessed. Your understanding of your instrument and of the three pieces studied will also be assessed through your appraisals of performing and composing, and through the composition brief.

Further composing

Composition 2 must be related to one of the core styles in Areas of Study 3 (Dance Music) or 4 (Traditions and Innovation). As with Composition 1, you will have to design a brief for your piece. The brief must state on what aspects of the core styles you are basing your composition.

Don't worry if you look at the list of core styles and don't know anything about them. Your GCSE course will help you to identify composing techniques from these styles, and you will be able to relate these techniques to your other musical interests. There are plenty of suggestions for starting points for composing in the chapters on Areas of Study 3 and 4.

Assessment

It is useful to know how your compositions will be marked as this

Imagine that you are a singer and are composing a song for a musical about a character who has discovered that their partner has been unfaithful. You use many of the conventions of the popular song: verse/chorus structure; an instrumental solo; an accompaniment for piano, rhythm guitar, bass and drums. So far you have followed the conventions of the style you are basing your piece on. You might challenge those conventions by having the last chorus interrupted by the sounds of a siren and dialogue as the police arrive – at the very end of the song the listeners realise that the singer has killed his or her unfaithful partner. You will have shown consistency in using the standard songwriting forms but will have used them in a very individual way.

One third of the marks for Composition 1 are given for how well your piece shows you have understood the music you have studied in Area of Study 1 (Exploiting the Resource).

One third of the marks for Composition 2 are given for how well your piece shows you have understood the music you have studied in either Area of Study 3 (Dance Music) or Area of Study 4 (Traditions and Innovation).

Composition 1

Warning. Photocopying any part of this book without permission is illegal.

can have a big impact on how you set about your work. Each piece is marked out of 15. There are 10 marks for how successful the composition is as a piece in its own right (the common criteria) and 5 for the extent to which you have understood the music explored in the Areas of Study and have fulfilled your composing briefs. For Composition 1, further marks are awarded for the brief and for your appraisal of the composition.

To get a good mark for the common criteria you will need to:

✦ Show imaginative development of musical ideas

✦ Show consistency and individuality in the way you follow and challenge the conventions on which the piece is based. This means that you should base your composing on the conventions of a particular musical style, but should also be able to challenge those conventions (see *left*).

✦ Use musical devices, and combine and manipulate them successfully within a well-defined structure

✦ Create a strong sense of personal style.

To get a good mark for Composition 1 you will need to:

✦ Design the music well for your own instrument or voice, showing understanding of a range of techniques of composing for it

✦ Show an in-depth understanding of the selected features from the three pieces that you have studied

✦ Successfully combine those musical features and techniques with your own musical style

✦ Create a successful piece of music that achieves what you set out in your brief.

To get a good mark for Composition 2 you will need to:

✦ Use a range of features and composing techniques from one of the core styles

✦ Combine these features with your own personal musical style

✦ Fully meet the stylistic intentions set out in your brief.

The brief

You will be assessed on the extent to which your composition does what you say it is going to do in the brief. This means that you should think very carefully before writing the brief.

The quality of the brief itself is assessed for Composition 1. To get a good mark here your brief will need to show that you are designing your composition around features chosen from the three pieces that you have studied. Show that you are making intelligent musical decisions about particular instrumental or vocal techniques that you intend to use. Have a look at the brief printed on page 27. Imagine that you are a pianist and that you have chosen to study three pieces in the jazz piano genre.

> These are the three pieces from the same genre – jazz piano – that you have chosen to study.

Composition 1

Instrument: piano
Focus for study: jazz piano

Three pieces studied (the first is also to be performed for assessment as Performance 1:

1. Main title music to *The Firm* (Dave Grusin)
2. *All Blues* (Miles Davis) from the Associated Board Jazz Piano books
3. *It's a Raggy Waltz* (Dave Brubeck).

Brief

To compose a jazz piece for piano with saxophone to represent a city atmosphere that:

✦ Uses these features of the piano-writing in *The Firm*: pounding ostinato bass; off-beat chords with added notes; the blues scale; tremolo; and crushed notes

✦ Uses the tune–solos–tune structure heard on the recordings of *All Blues* and *Raggy Waltz*

✦ Has a bass and drum backing, so that the piano doesn't have to play the bass line all the time (as in the original versions of *All Blues* and *Raggy Waltz*).

> Your brief must relate to the instrument that you have studied and used for Performance 1.

> You are showing that you have made decisions about specific instrumental techniques to use and that they are related to the music you have studied.

> You are demonstrating your understanding by using specific musical processes from the three pieces that you have studied.

For Composition 2 you need to write a brief based around one of the core styles from Areas of Study 3 or 4. It is essential that you identify in this brief the core style (or composing techniques from that style) that your composition is based on.

Your teacher (and perhaps an external moderator) will read your brief when your work is marked – this will show them your intentions and how you planned to develop your musical ideas. It is really worth trying to write an imaginative initial brief. The sections of this book on the Areas of Study suggest several possible starting points for compositions based around these core styles, and these could be adapted as briefs. Look through these suggestions and then think about how these styles can interact with your own musical interests. Be imaginative in thinking about how you can use a range of features from one of the core styles in a way that reflects your own musical personality.

You may think that having to work to a brief (especially one related to a particular style of music) will tie you down too much. However many composers find that the more restrictions they place on themselves the more it helps to get their ideas flowing. Imagine for a moment you can compose anything you want in any style with any instruments or voices. How are you going to start? You could spend hours, days or weeks staring at a blank piece of paper or computer screen. Now imagine that you are going to compose a piece in a minimalist style for yourself and two friends in your GCSE group. You immediately have several starting points here: you need to find out about some minimalist techniques and you need to find out what your friends can do musically.

As you work on your piece you may find that your original intentions change. This is acceptable as long as:

✦ You keep a record of the original intentions and any changes that you make

Composition 2

Suggestions for starting points for Composition 2 can be found on:

Page 76 pavan/galliard

Page 79 waltz

Page 83 disco

Page 90 salsa

Page 96 bhangra

Page 100 minimalism.

For Composition 2, if you set out to write a waltz for three woodwind instruments, but then change it to a waltz for piano, this is fine (since the waltz is a core style). But if you decide that you want to change it to a march for three woodwind instruments you risk losing five marks since a march is not a core style.

Composing 27

♦ The features of the core styles from the Areas of Study are still there in the finished version.

Composing, improvising and the Terminal Task

Practising for the Terminal Task (see page 37) can also help you to get going with your other composing. Use one of the music examples on page 40 as a starting point – force yourself to come up with a piece in only 25 minutes. Your teacher will be able to provide you with more starting points. This is a particularly useful technique if you take a lot of time to get started on a composition.

Make a habit of 'doodling' with your instrument or voice. Improvising in this way can result in many good ideas – you may well not like what you come up with, but equally you might discover an idea that will have potential for development or growth. Write down or record any good ideas before you forget them.

It is also worth improvising in a group. This is a good way in which to find out about the sounds and capabilities of different instruments and voices.

What next?

The composer Danny Elfman came up with the idea for the 1989 Batman film theme while on an aeroplane – he had to go to the aircraft toilet to hum his ideas into a tape recorder before he forgot them.

Form and structure

Most good pieces of music have a clear shape or form. Artists such as painters and potters can stand back and look at the overall shape of their work, but this is harder for musicians because music exists in time. To judge if your compositions have a good sense of structure you really need to hear them performed. This way you can spot if some sections are too long or too short, or if you use the same idea so many times that it becomes boring.

You will encounter several standard musical forms in Area of Study 2. You will also look at the way music is structured in the core styles from Areas of Study 3 and 4. It may well help you to use some of these forms in your own music, but do so as a starting point and not as a kind of jelly mould. If you are going to employ a standard form such as ternary, rondo or variation, try to combine the basic structure with some of your own ideas.

A piece in ternary form has the structure:

A	B	A
(first idea)	(new idea)	(first idea again)

You could make this more interesting by:

♦ Varying the A section when it comes back

♦ Combining elements of tune A and B in the final section (or in a coda added after the third section).

It is important to have an overall picture of your piece. Many GCSE composers start at bar 1, then go on to bar 2, then bar 3 and so on. The trouble with this approach is that it makes it difficult to gain an overview of the piece. One of the best composers at building satisfying musical forms was Beethoven. He would often place a tiny musical idea near the start of a piece. At first it doesn't seem to have any significance but later it becomes all important. Try to think about how each small musical idea fits in to the big picture.

Beginnings and endings are important. What is the first thing the

Warning. Photocopying any part of this book without permission is illegal.

28 Composing

listeners will hear? Will the piece end with a fade-out or a dramatic climax? It is sometimes helpful to compose the end (or the climax) of a piece first and then work out how to get to that point.

Once you have invented a good musical idea, what do you do next?

Developing your initial ideas

- Repeat the idea exactly? The piece may sound boring if you do this too much. But bringing ideas back later on does help to give a sense of shape to the piece.

- Change or develop the idea? Try some of these suggestions: write a rhythmic or melodic variation; transpose the idea; add (or change) chords; add a countermelody; use different sounds (instruments, voices or music technology); use more (or fewer) instruments or voices; vary the texture; use the idea backwards or upside down; transform part of your idea into something new; play your idea faster or slower; use minimalist techniques (see page 97); use space – try bouncing your idea between two separate groups of musicians, or use music technology to pan the idea between speakers; alter the actual sounds that you use – try mutes, effects (FX) and so on.

- Move on to a new idea? The piece may seem bitty if you have too many ideas. Think about how different your new idea will be. It will need to have some contrast, but if it is completely different in style the piece may sound disjointed.

Try to combine these approaches and make sure you are using composing techniques that you have come across in the Areas of Study. Above all, try to have an overview of the piece:

- What sort of music do you want to compose? Imagine people listening to your piece. How do you want them to react?

- Where is the piece going? Where does the part that you are working on fit within the overall shape of the piece? How does the shape of your piece compare with music that you have explored in the Areas of Study?

- Where is the most important point in the piece? How can you make this moment stand out?

Trying out your work

Evaluating your work should be a natural part of composing. If you listen to it regularly and change sections that are not working, the piece is likely to be much more successful.

When you hear your composition, ask yourself:

- Does it have the effect you want?

- Is the balance wrong in places, meaning that perhaps the tune is not heard clearly?

- Do some of your harmonies clash in ways that you did not intend?

- Does the structure hold together convincingly?

- Is there enough variety of timbre and texture?

Get feedback from your performers. What did they feel worked well, less well or not at all? They will quickly be able to point out

Warning. Photocopying any part of this book without permission is illegal.

difficulties and you can revise these sections as necessary. Make a note of their comments so that you can use them in your evaluation of the composition. It is worth recording your piece at this stage to help you appraise it and make revisions.

When you next try out your piece concentrate on any sections that you have revised. Do they work now, or do you need to adjust them still further? Chiselling away at music in this way is constructive – imagine yourself as a sculptor, gradually shaping a piece of stone.

Even if nobody else is involved in performing your composition, it is still important for you to try out your music in front of others as this can help you evaluate it. Apart from getting useful feedback, you may hear your piece differently when others are listening.

Start your compositions early so that you have time to perform and revise them. Most importantly, try to finish first drafts early enough for you to leave them alone for several days (or even weeks) and then come back to the music with fresh ears. Making clear judgements about your own work when you have just finished composing is hard to do.

Appraising skills

For Composition 1 you have to produce a formal appraisal, and this is assessed as part of your coursework. Your appraisal can be written or recorded – choose the format that suits you best. Appraisal of Composition 2 is not assessed, but you should still produce a description of the composing process and an evaluation of the finished piece.

As explained on page 22, appraisal is not a matter of saying 'my composition worked well… I was very pleased with my piece… it was excellent'. You need to show critical judgement and include much more detail than this. Build your appraisal around answers to these questions:

- To what extent did you meet the demands of the brief? (Point out specific features of your piece that relate to the brief.)
- Did you make any changes to the brief? If so, why?
- What features of the piece work well?
- What parts of the piece are you unhappy with?
- What problems did you encounter during the composing process?
- What would you improve if you had more time?
- What did you learn from trying out your piece?
- If you have submitted both a score and recording, which of these shows your intentions best?

For Composition 1:

- How do the musical features of your composition relate to the three pieces that you studied (including your Performance 1)?
- What instrumental (or vocal) techniques did you use? How do these relate to techniques in the three pieces that you studied?

For Composition 2:

✦ Which of the core styles from Areas of Study 3 and 4 does your piece relate to?

✦ What composing techniques from this style have you used in your piece?

The craft of composing

Some people imagine that composers suddenly receive inspiration in a flash of lightning and that's it – end of story. If only it were that easy! For most people, composing is like Thomas Edison's description of genius – one per cent inspiration and 99 per cent perspiration. The 99 per cent is something that can be learned. Don't keep waiting for inspiration until the night before your GCSE coursework is due in.

A large part of the craft of composing is knowing how to create music that suits particular instruments and performers. Area of Study 1 deals with exploiting the resource of your own instrument or voice. In some ways this is the easy bit – you know what *you* can or cannot do. Hopefully your compositions will also involve other performers, so you also need to learn how to compose effectively for them.

It is probably best to compose for people in your class, or in an ensemble in which you regularly perform. The vital thing is to write for people who will be around for the entire length of the composing process and have time to try out several different drafts of your piece. It is also worth composing for people that you know to be reliable. It is even better if you can compose music to be performed at a particular event – this is a real incentive to get on with your work.

A good starting point is to find out about the capabilities of the instruments, voices or technology that you are composing for. Speak to performers and find out the range of each instrument. Ask what your friends find easy to play and what is difficult for their instrument or voice. Some keys are particularly difficult for certain instruments, for example.

Keys with sharps (such as D major) tend to suit string instruments and keys with flats (such as B♭ major) are usually easier for brass, clarinet and saxophone players.

Don't worry if the people that you want to compose for aren't very experienced as musicians. The secret is to find out what they can do well and then make use of these strengths in your piece.

Texture

Imagine that you have decided to compose a waltz for a clarinet group in your school. It would make sense to go along to rehearsals to listen to other pieces for this particular group. Notice how vital it is to vary the textures in an ensemble. GCSE composers frequently forget this. A common weakness is always to assign the tune to the top part (clarinet I in this case). Split the melodic ideas among as many parts as possible. Everyone likes to play the tune. Use rests to break up the textures – these are particularly vital so that wind players can breathe.

Experiment with different textures. You might try:

✦ Full, thick textures, with everyone playing

✦ Thin textures, with only one or two instruments at a time

- High sounds answering low sounds in a call-and-response style
- Having one instrument play the tune while the others play long, held notes (or a drone)
- Having instruments imitate each other.

Music technology

You can use music technology in several ways. You could:

- Design your Composition 2 purely for music technology resources using a sequencer
- Use a multitrack tape recorder to build up a composition in layers
- Compose a piece to be performed by a combination of live players/singers and music technology
- Use music technology as a tool to help you compose a piece for live performers.

You are encouraged to use ICT but it is not a requirement. The GCSE listening exam is likely to include questions that require you to demonstrate an understanding of the impact of ICT on music. The more you use music technology as part of your course, the more easily you will be able to answer these questions. You don't gain any credit simply for using ICT. However you will get credit for any creativity that you show in using music technology as part of the composing process.

If you do compose a piece purely for music technology, then make sure you exploit the resource of technology in the same way that you would for an instrument or voice. If you are using a sequencer make full use of its features. A sequencer allows you to choose appropriate sounds, get the balance right between different parts, quantise notes so that rhythms are correct, pan the sounds between left and right speaker and, in many cases, add effects (FX).

If you use music technology to help compose a piece for live performers make sure that you keep the needs of real people in mind throughout. Your synthesiser or computer soundcard can produce a sound like a trumpet, but it will probably not warn you that you have written notes that are too high for your trumpet-playing friend, or that you have demanded the impossible and asked a single trumpeter to play a chord. It certainly will not remind you that your trumpet part has continued for several minutes without a single breathing point. Nor will it tell you how long a rest you need for the player to fit a mute or turn a page.

If you use a sequencer make sure that you save your work regularly and keep back-up copies. Remember that if you are relying on using equipment in school there is likely to be a queue to use it in the weeks leading up to the GCSE hand-in date. In other words if you are going to use music technology start early.

A word of warning for composers using samples or material downloaded from the Internet. This is common in some musical styles (bhangra, for example). Compositions consisting entirely of samples of music by other people are treated as arrangements (see page 33) and the examiners will expect you to provide significant creative input of your own beyond merely cutting and pasting them together. The same advice applies if you make use of one of the many computer programs (such as *Dance eJay*) that contain pre-recorded samples designed to fit with each other. If you do base a piece on borrowed material in this way, make sure that you use the material creatively in combination with your own musical ideas. You are strongly advised to provide a full account of your own input so it can be properly credited.

Any material used which is not your own *must* be acknowledged and copies of the original material handed in with your composition (for example, recordings of the individual samples used). You should also say where you found the material that you have borrowed (for example, a web site address). It is only acceptable to use the music of other composers in compositions if this is acknowledged.

Warning. Photocopying any part of this book without permission is illegal.

Arrangements

You have the option to produce an arrangement of an existing piece instead of an original composition. You should think carefully before choosing to do this. It may seem at first as though this is an easy option, but it really isn't. Whatever piece you choose to arrange, you will need to hand in the source material – the printed music or recording that you used as the basis for your arrangement. This is to make it possible to assess what *your* creative input has been. To do well, an arrangement must show a large element of your own creativity.

Look at your finished arrangement and imagine it with everything that came from the original source material taken out. What would be left that is yours? It is important to ask yourself this question because it is what is left that will be assessed. If all you do is rewrite the original piece for different musical forces you will not get good marks at GCSE.

Ways to show your own creative input in an arrangement:

- Combine your own musical ideas with the original material (for example, invent countermelodies to go with a salsa tune)
- Invent new harmonies
- Create new textures – for example, don't just copy the um-cha-cha accompaniment of *The Blue Danube* waltz, but write your own accompaniment figures
- Invent new tunes to fit with the chords of the original piece
- Change the style of the piece
- Invent a new structure for the work, with your own introduction, ending and linking sections
- Rethink the style of the accompaniment so that it really suits the instruments, voices or music technology for which you are producing the arrangement.

Above all, make sure that the arrangement is as much about you as about the original piece.

Joint compositions

You have the option to submit a joint composition for Composition 2 – this is the one that must be based around Areas of Study 3 and 4. You may well have done a lot of group composing at Key Stage 3 and this may seem like an attractive option. However, you are strongly advised to avoid joint compositions if you possibly can.

If you submit a joint composition you must make it clear which parts of the piece *you* composed. You might for example have written the melody line for the first section and the chords for the second section. You will only get credit for the parts of the piece you can identify as material that you created.

Presentation

Your compositions may be submitted in recorded and/or written form. You will learn most if you produce both a recording and a score, although either one is acceptable on its own. If you do

Warning. Photocopying any part of this book without permission is illegal.

submit both written and recorded versions you should indicate which best represents your intentions. It may be that you have produced a detailed score but the recorded performance didn't go well. This is fine – indicate that the score shows your intentions better than the recording. On the other hand, perhaps you recorded your piece in layers, and only thought about writing it out later. You have made a good attempt at notating difficult rhythms, but you are not sure that you have got them exactly right. Your recording is good however so indicate that this shows your intentions better than the score. You are strongly advised not to hand in a written score that you have been unable to try out with the intended musical forces. It is vital that you hear the sound of your piece – composing is not a paper exercise.

The sessions when you record your piece can be the most rewarding parts of the GCSE course. You can record your music yourself or involve friends or your teacher. If you do need others to help perform your music, make sure that they have rehearsal material well in advance. This might consist of written music or perhaps a tape of your piece for them to rehearse with.

It is in your interests to give your performers detailed instructions about how to play your piece. You may have a friend who is a brilliant improviser on electric guitar and it may be tempting to ask him/her to do a solo as part of your piece. Bear in mind that you will not get credit for your friend's solo unless you can demonstrate that you have shown him/her exactly what to play.

If you have composed music for a group you will hopefully have tried the music out with your friends at earlier stages in the composing process. Do rehearse thoroughly before you try to record. If your piece is at all complicated it may well take some time to get it together – remember that you know how it should sound, but your performers don't have this inside knowledge of the piece. Think back to the last time you went to a rehearsal. Did the music you were rehearsing work first time? It is unlikely that it did. You needed to rehearse it properly, and the same applies to your own composition.

For Composition 1 you will have to submit the composing brief and your appraisal of the finished composition (together with your appraisal of Performance 1).

For Composition 2 you will have to give details of your composing brief (and any changes made during the composing process) on a Candidate Intentions Form. You must show how your brief relates to one of the core styles from Areas of Study 3 or 4. You should also write a short description of the composing process and an evaluation of the finished composition, although this is not formally assessed in the same way as Composition 1.

You must include details of any music technology used and any material taken from an outside source (for example samples, MIDI files and arrangement sources).

Scores Scores may consist of staff notation or a chord progression with lyrics. They could take the form of a chart, like those in the jazz *Real Books*, or a leadsheet, based on the melody-with-chords format employed in the *Busker's Books*. If you choose a less detailed type of notation (common in popular music) remember to show how the sections (verses and choruses) follow one another rather than simply typing out the lyrics with chord symbols. You are strongly advised to record your piece as well as producing a score.

Warning. Photocopying any part of this book without permission is illegal.

For some types of music you may want to write a graphic score. If you do this, make sure that it includes detailed directions to the performers – remember you cannot receive credit for other people's contributions to your piece.

Computer-generated scores are acceptable but should be neatly formatted and edited so they are readable. Don't assume that if you play something into a computer sequencer it will automatically produce a perfect score. The software will record *exactly* what you play. If this is translated literally into notation the result may be as confused and unreadable as the top stave *below* (the first phrase of *Twinkle, twinkle little star*):

Note that any composition that is not in conventional staff notation must be recorded.

Fortunately sequencing software has tools to edit scores. In the lower stave *above*, the computer has been told to move all the notes to the nearest crotchet beat and to adjust their lengths to crotchets (or multiples of crotchets). This is called quantising to ¼ notes (or to '4') and is just one of the types of editing you may need to do in order to produce an acceptable score. If you intend to use a computer to produce a printed score you will need to spend some time getting to know how the software works.

In general computer sequencing software such as the Cubase and Logic families are most useful for composing and manipulating sounds. Specialist score-writing packages such as Sibelius and Finale are probably easier to use if your main purpose is to produce a written score.

Recordings may be on cassette tape or CD. If you make a live recording you should carry out a sound check. You may have to move microphones around so that everything can be picked up clearly. If you are making a live recording with only one microphone then you will have to position your performers carefully so that the balance of the parts is right. Before you start recording, ask your performers to play as loudly as possible so that you can set the recording level. If you set the level too low you will get poor sound (with lots of hiss if you are recording to tape). If you set it too high you will get distortion. Bear in mind that performers may play even louder in the real performance. A clear, well-balanced recording will be important and may be the best guide to your work, especially in popular music and jazz where the score might be rather sketchy or where there is no score at all.

Recordings
Although the actual recording is not assessed, getting a good-quality recording will be very satisfying for you and will help your piece to make a good impression.

Here are some suggestions to help you make better recordings:

✦ Avoid using a tape recorder with automatic gain control – allowing levels to be set automatically will remove some of the dynamic contrast from the recording.

✦ Record several versions and check them. Can you hear all the tracks/parts? Are any distorted? Is the recording balanced between left- and right-hand speakers?

✦ You can often use equalisation (EQ) to reduce hiss or bring out an instrument.

✦ You can use the pan controls to place instruments in the left/right mix.

Warning. Photocopying any part of this book without permission is illegal.

♦ Vocals, piano, drums and solo instruments usually sound better if a little reverberation is added. Always record tracks without special effects and add them later.

♦ If you are using a computer timbre and it sounds a little thin, try copying the track and transposing the copy up or down an octave (or delaying it a fraction). When added to the original track this should help thicken the sound. You can also try adding an effect such as chorus.

Your composition

You should always seek advice about your composing, but you don't necessarily have to act on it. Some of the best-known films, songs, books and plays would never have come into existence if people had taken notice of all the advice they had been given. You should always listen to what people say and think about it carefully, because they are trying to help you. You may end up agreeing with the advice, or you may disagree with it. If the advice is a matter of opinion and you feel strongly that what you have composed is really what you want, then stick with it. Only *you* can make final decisions about your composing – nobody can compose your piece for you.

Warning. Photocopying any part of this book without permission is illegal.

Terminal Task: Respond and Communicate

The title for this part of the GCSE examination sounds a bit lethal, but 'terminal task' only really means that the task takes place at the end of the course.

The Terminal Task lasts for only 30 minutes and it would be easy to see this as a minor part of the exam. This would be a mistake: 15% of the entire marks for the GCSE rest on this one section. This means that you would be well advised to spend a significant amount of time practising for the Terminal Task during the earlier part of your course.

In the exam, you will be given a sheet containing three musical starting points (or *stimuli*) and you will then have 25 minutes to prepare a piece of music based on *one* of these. You can see some examples of these stimuli on page 40 (although obviously these aren't the ones that you will get in the actual exam).

How will you know which stimulus to choose? In the exam you can ask your teacher to play any of the three stimuli (starting points) so that you can hear what they sound like before choosing one. When you have chosen, your teacher can play your choice twice more, and you are allowed to record this (so that you can listen to it during the preparation period). You would be well advised to do so, especially if you don't read music fluently. Be sure to check carefully that you have got the stimulus correct and that you haven't let it mutate into something else during the preparation time, as this could make it difficult for you to get a good mark.

At the end of the 25-minute preparation time, you will need to present your finished composition. You have a choice of three ways in which to do this:

✦ Perform the piece live

✦ Perform the piece using music technology

✦ Hand in a written-down version of the piece.

You are allowed to use any instrument (or instruments), voice, ICT, music technology, recording or writing equipment during the examination. You can record part or all of your work during the 25-minute preparation time. Whichever option you choose, at the end of the preparation time you will have a maximum of five minutes to record a performance of the piece or to finish writing it down. Note that you are not allowed to bring in any pre-prepared work – the entire piece must be composed during the examination time.

The Terminal Task and Area of Study 2

It is important to realise that your Terminal Task composition must contain some melodic invention. The reason for this is that the terminal task relates to Area of Study 2 (Techniques of Melodic Composition) – and you will need to be able to show in your composition that you can use some of the melodic techniques that you have studied. This means that if you choose the chord

---

You will have a choice of three stimuli to base your music on:

✦ A rhythm pattern

✦ A note pattern

✦ A chord sequence.

Your teacher is allowed to transpose the stimuli into keys that suit your instrument or voice better or to write them out in a different form of notation (such as steel pan or Indian notation) if this is more helpful for you.

If you play a non-melodic instrument such as drum kit or rhythm guitar, you will need to think carefully about how best to tackle the terminal task. If you play a second, melodic instrument it might be worth using it for this part of the exam. Alternatively, you might want to use music technology or write your piece down. A good option for a rhythm guitarist might be to use a multi-track tape recorder to record a backing based around the given chord sequence and then to improvise melodic ideas on top, perhaps using a different instrument.

sequence, it will not be enough just to play the chords through a few times in different rhythm patterns (or grooves) – you will need to invent melodies to fit with, or between, the given chords. If you choose the rhythm pattern, you will need to turn it into a melody.

One of the best ways to prepare is to study techniques of melodic composition and apply these to various stimuli. The example *left* shows how a given rhythmic pattern has been transformed into a melody and how a variety of techniques can then be applied to the melody.

Of course, if all you do is play about with different melodic techniques you may end up with a dry exercise rather than a piece of music. Use these techniques to generate new musical ideas, but then think how you can assemble these ideas into a coherent piece of music.

Although you only have 25 minutes to prepare, it is still important to produce a piece with a satisfying shape. You could think about using one of the musical forms you have studied in Area of Study 2. You might, for example, use:

1. Ternary form (ABA). Use your chosen stimulus as the basis for the main musical idea. After you have explored this for a short while invent a new musical idea for the middle section (perhaps by using part of the stimulus in a different way). End the piece by returning to your opening material.

2. Rondo (ABACA etc). Here you will also use your chosen stimulus as the basis for your main musical idea, but this time invent several other short ideas (related to parts of the stimulus) and alternate them with your main idea.

3. The structure of Indian classical music. You might start with a section in which you explore the given note pattern very slowly and in free time, perhaps over a drone. This could then lead to a faster section where you explore the note pattern in a more rhythmic manner, and you might end with a fast, free improvisation.

It doesn't really matter what form you use, but it will help you to tackle the Terminal Task and to communicate the essence of your piece much better if you have a clear overview of where the piece is heading (see page 28 for more information on this).

How to prepare for the Terminal Task

Decide whether you should go for live performance, music-technology performance or the written option. Experiment with different ways of tackling the specimen tasks on page 40 and decide which is best for you to use in the real exam. It is important to try doing these mock Terminal Tasks under the same time constraints that you will have in the real exam, so that you can find out how long it takes you to use music technology, for example, or to write your ideas down. You only have 25 minutes – you will need to practise working fast.

Warning. Photocopying any part of this book without permission is illegal.

How to get a good mark for the Terminal Task

Another name for the Terminal Task is 'Respond and Communicate', and assessment comes under these two headings. There are twice as many marks for the responding section as for communicating.

To get a good mark for responding to the chosen stimulus, you will need to produce a piece that:

- Is clearly related to the stimulus
- Uses musical devices and techniques (as studied in Area of Study 2)
- Has a clear and effective structure
- Is imaginative and has a sense of style.

You may wonder how close your piece has to be to the chosen stimulus. One extreme would be for you to stick so closely to the stimulus that you do almost nothing else except repeat it and consequently the piece quickly becomes boring. The other extreme would be for you to move so far away that the original stimulus gets forgotten. In either case, you are unlikely to get a good mark. Instead use the stimulus as the basis for your music but use the techniques that you have explored in Area of Study 2 to vary and develop the original idea. It is not a question of just repeating the stimulus, but of seeing what you can draw out of it.

The mark for **communicating** is about how effectively you use either live performance, music technology or notation to communicate to somebody else what your music is about. To get a good mark you will need to:

- Perform expressively and with a sense of style OR
- Use music technology to produce a performance that is expressive and stylish OR
- Write down your music in such a way that it communicates clearly, and includes sufficient details to allow another musician to perform the piece in a stylish and expressive manner (eg tempo markings, dynamics, phrasing etc).

In each case, to get a good mark, you must move beyond simply performing or writing down the bare notes and rhythms. If you have thought about the mood or atmosphere that you want to create while preparing the piece this should help you to communicate it in a stylish and expressive manner.

Above all, don't think of the Terminal Task as a technical exercise, but practise making your compositions into real pieces of music with strong characters of their own. Use pauses and rests for dramatic effect. Record your practice pieces – do they sound interesting? Make your pieces sad, funny, military, ballad-like, jazzy, aggressive, dramatic – anything as long as they aren't bland and boring! If you work in this way, practising for the terminal task can also make an excellent starting point for your coursework composing.

Warning. Photocopying any part of this book without permission is illegal.

Terminal Task: Specimen Sheet 1

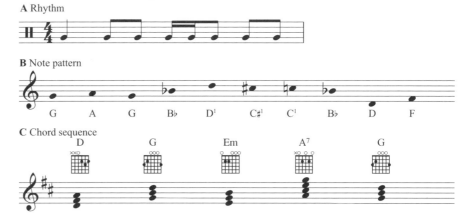

Terminal Task: Specimen Sheet 2

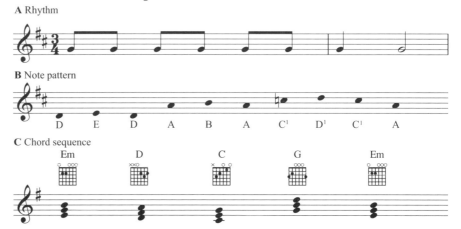

Terminal Task: Specimen Sheet 3

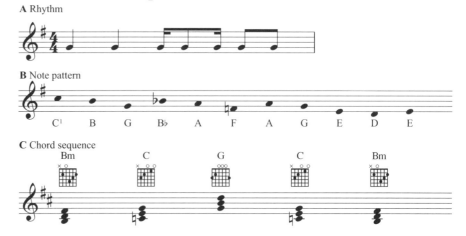

Warning. Photocopying any part of this book without permission is illegal.

Exploiting the Resource

For this Area of Study you must choose, with assistance from your teacher, three related pieces for your instrument. Through studying these works in detail you will learn how composers have written effectively for your instrument and how you can do the same in your own composing. It is absolutely essential to select the works with great care because:

- You will have to perform one of the three pieces, so you will need to make sure that it is of a standard that will allow you to show what you can do without it being too difficult for you

- One of your compositions will need to reflect what you have learnt about the potential of your instrument by using some of the techniques from the pieces you have studied.

The success of your work will be tested in:

- Your Performance 1 and your appraisal of that performance
- Your brief for Composition 1, the composition itself and your appraisal of that composition.

We have given some advice on selecting suitable music on page 19. In this chapter we are going to concentrate on how you should go about studying the pieces. This doesn't mean learning facts such as the dates of composers or the number of top 20 hits by the band concerned. It means understanding what is 'going on' in a piece of music – how the composer is using your instrument and what the performer is trying to convey, how an atmosphere is created, how a sense of style is achieved, why matters such as contrast, good tone or raw energy are essential to some types of music and yet irrelevant to others. Above all, it is about how your instrument is used not merely to play notes, but to create effective music. All of this will need some research, as we shall see.

In order to produce a good brief and appraisals you will need to be able to write about music in a clear and expert style. As we go through this chapter we shall explain various technical terms that you may find useful. Terminology often allows you to explain what you mean in just a word or two, instead of having to write long and complex sentences. But terminology used incorrectly is worse than useless so, if in doubt, explain what you mean in plain but precise English when writing your brief and appraisals.

To discover what is meant by 'exploiting the resource' we need to look at some examples of actual music. It would take too much space to consider every possible instrument so we will confine detailed discussion to selected pieces from Schumann's *Album for the Young*. This collection of short piano works started life in 1848 as a present for the composer's daughter, who was learning the piano. Its contents have been used as teaching (and exam!) pieces for more than 150 years and have often been arranged for other instruments. So while some of our discussion will be particular to piano music, other points will be more general. You and your teachers should hopefully be able to apply the examples we have given to other types of instrumental music.

Again we have used the term 'instrument' to include the voice in this chapter.

Warning. Photocopying any part of this book without permission is illegal.

Melodie

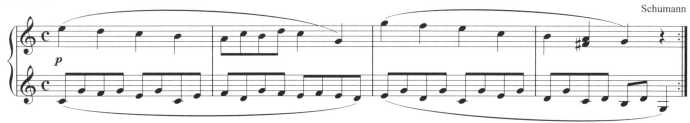

The German title tells us that this piece is all about melody. In fact it is like a song without any words. There is a clear tune in the top part (played with the right hand) and a distinct accompaniment in the lower part (played with the left hand).

The melody sounds like a song because it moves mainly by **step** and the phrase marks indicate that it is to be performed **legato** (smoothly). It is easy to imagine a singer taking a breath at the end of bar 2 (where the phrase mark ends) and during the rest in bar 4.

The terms **compass** and **range** both refer to the total span of pitches in a melody or on an instrument.

Schumann's melody also resembles vocal music because it has a limited **range** – from G to G an octave higher in the extract above. This would fit easily within the **compass** of a soprano (treble) voice.

The word **character** is useful to use when you want to refer to the overall mood of a short piece.

Listen to this extract and decide what sort of **character** you feel it conveys to the listener. Do you agree that it is peaceful? Several factors contribute to this:

The term **dynamics** refers to the relative levels of loudness and quietness in music.

◆ The only dynamic indicated is *p* (quiet)

◆ The legato phrases fall from high to low

◆ The rhythms are formed from just crotchets and quavers

◆ The accompaniment consists of gently-flowing quavers.

Register is just one particular part of the full compass of an instrument. Often we refer to high, middle and low registers, but on some instruments particular registers have special names.

Notice that the left hand is in the middle **register** of the piano. It is in the treble clef (rather than the more usual bass clef) and is mostly above middle C. This helps to give the music its delicacy but pianists have to be careful that such high accompaniments do not become more prominent than the tune.

Texture refers to the number of simultaneous parts in a composition and how they relate to each other. It is also used to refer to tone colour (eg a string texture, a low texture).

Finally, the music has a thin **texture**. There is mainly one note at a time in the right hand and one note at a time in the left. We could describe this as a two-part texture since there are normally just two musical parts sounding together. We could also identify the texture of this particular extract as melody-and-accompaniment, since this describes the functions of the two parts.

We can see that there is much to investigate in even just four bars of music. We have seen that the pianist has two jobs – not only to play the tune, but also to accompany it. This is perhaps the main way in which Schumann has exploited the piano in this piece.

We have also provided some pointers to how the music might be performed to best effect. To achieve a song-like quality the melody will need good, even tone with a fair amount of finger-weight so that the notes really sing out. Thinking of where a singer might breathe will help shape the phrases. The accompaniment needs to be very even; it has twice as many notes as the melody and will need to be very discreet if it is not to over-balance the tune.

Warning. Photocopying any part of this book without permission is illegal.

42   Exploiting the Resource

Our discussion should also have given you a number of ideas for achieving a peaceful mood in your own compositions. And above all it will have shown you a little of how to write about music in your brief and appraisals.

We do not have the space to deal with every example in such detail but it should be obvious that the second piece from *Album for the Young* provides a vivid contrast to *Melodie*.

Soldatenmarsch

Instead of the quiet, dreamy, legato style of *Melodie*, Schumann's 'soldier's march' is loud, precise and military. The dotted rhythm at the start of each four-bar phrase gives the music a strong sense of forward movement. But this is not a grand march – most chords are followed by a quaver rest, making the piece sound rather clipped – perhaps these are toy soldiers?

The only dynamic used by Schumann in this piece is *f*, which he added at the start of most four-bar phrases, almost like a reminder in case the pianist had faded away in the preceding phrase. In fact, if you like the 'toy soldiers' idea you could deliberately **diminuendo** (gradually get quieter) in each phrase, as if the soldiers are circling around a toy castle – alternately disappearing and then manically reappearing every four seconds! Certainly any performance would benefit from some imaginative contrast in the dynamics.

The texture is mainly three part and can be described as **homophonic**, meaning that one part (the tune) has all the melodic interest while the other notes provide a simple accompaniment.

In this piece Schumann is exploiting the piano's ability to produce crisp, percussive tone. To convey the mood of a march the tempo will need military precision and the notes of the chords will need real unanimity of attack – remain alert and think of the sergeant major breathing down your neck as you play!

Ein Choral

A chorale is a German hymn tune harmonised for four-part choir (soprano, alto, tenor and bass voices). This is reflected in the four-part texture of the music. Schumann even writes the pairs of parts with stems in opposite directions, so we can imagine the notes sung by each voice part in the choir. This piece clearly exploits the piano's facility to play chords. For the performer one of the most important things is to ensure that it really does convey an

> **Warning.** Photocopying any part of this book without permission is illegal.

Exploiting the Resource

impression of religious vocal music. To do this, all parts (especially the melody) need to be legato and well phrased. That is not easy to achieve when simultaneously playing two notes in each hand throughout the piece. The **fermata** signs (⌒) indicate pauses – places where you should linger briefly – and in this piece they also mark the ends of phrases.

Jägerliedchen

Fresh and cheerful

Schumann

There is almost no movement by step in this extract. The tune moves mainly in **leaps** and since most of it is based on the notes of the triad of F major, we can say that it is a **triadic** melody.

Jägerliedchen means 'little hunting song'. Schumann sets the mood by using triadic figures that sound like the call of a huntsman's horn. With the exception of the C-major chord at the end of the first phrase, there is just a single unaccompanied melody in this extract. This is known as a **monophonic** texture. The two hands play this melody an octave apart – this is called **doubling** at the octave.

Listen to each hand separately and then together. You should be able to hear that each of the three versions of the melody has a different tone colour. In the same way a melody sung by women has a different tone colour from the same melody sung by men – and if this melody is sung by men and women in octaves, it will have yet a different quality.

This is an important point that can help your composing. There are not many instruments that easily enable a performer to double themselves, as you can on keyboard instruments. But if you are writing a piece for two or more players you can experiment with all sorts of doublings in order to produce different tone colours. For instance you could try flute and clarinet in octaves, or in **unison** (playing exactly the same notes) or even *two* octaves apart – the clarinet playing a tune in its lowest register with the flute playing the same tune two octaves higher.

If you prefer to leave it to the pianist to decide precisely how the sustaining pedal should be used in your composition you can write 'con ped.' (with pedal) below the lower stave at the start of the section in which you want the pedal to be used, and 'senza ped.' (without pedal) at the point where you wish the effect to cease.

Playing in octaves is not the only resource exploited by Schumann in this piece. The symbol ℘ℯ𝒹. directs the pianist to press the right-hand pedal, and the symbol ✱ shows where it is to be released. This device is often called the 'loud' or 'sustaining pedal' because it lifts the dampers on the piano's strings so that the sound sustains even after the keys are released. It makes the tone more resonant, and here Schumann might well have asked for its use because he wanted to conjure up a picture of horns sounding in an echoing forest.

Using the sustaining pedal to make notes ring on is very effective if all the notes affected are intended to be heard together, as with the tonic and dominant notes in this piece. But the sustaining pedal can easily be misused. For instance if it were held down throughout the phrases in *Ein Choral* the chords would blur into each other in a horribly discordant fashion. This would not be a good way to attempt legato playing!

Warning. Photocopying any part of this book without permission is illegal.

44 Exploiting the Resource

The left-hand pedal on the piano is often called the 'soft' pedal. While it does indeed quieten the sound, its main function is to produce a veiled tone. It does this on grand pianos by reducing the number of strings struck by the hammers. On upright pianos the pedal usually moves the hammers closer to the strings.

The term to indicate use of the 'soft' pedal is *una corda* ('one string'), and to abandon its use *tre corde* ('three strings').

Another resource exploited by Schumann in *Jägerliedchen* is the pressure-sensitive touch of the piano keyboard. At the start, accents (marked >) are used to show that the tonic notes are to be played with special emphasis, perhaps reminding us of the urgency of the hunt. This opening is followed by two bars of **staccato**, indicated by the dots above and below note heads. Performers might well decide to play these passages more quietly than the loud opening.

Staccato means that notes should be played shorter than their indicated lengths so that adjacent notes sound detached from each other. It is the opposite of the legato articulation we discussed on page 42.

Volksliedchen

Volksliedchen means 'little folk song' – the minor key and direction to play 'in a plaintive manner' indicate that this is a sad song. The texture is melody-and-accompaniment again, but here Schumann exploits a different piano technique. The opening melody is legato but its accompaniment is detached – a combination that requires good independence of hands from the pianist.

Another characteristic piano idiom in this extract is the use of arpeggiated (or 'spread') chords, indicated by the wavy vertical lines. In performance the notes of these chords are not sounded together. Instead they are played in rapid succession, from lowest to highest.

An idiom means a particular style of expression. We could say that Schumann's piano music is idiomatic piano music since it often exploits textures and techniques that particularly suit the piano.

The first two notes in the last bar are marked with staccato dots but are also joined with a slur. This type of articulation is known as semi-staccato and should sound midway between staccato and legato in effect.

Fröhlicher Landmann, von der Arbeit zurückkehrend

The title, which means 'The jolly farmhand, returning from work', gives a clear indication of the pastoral mood Schumann wants to portray. Like *Volksliedchen* the pianist needs to present a legato melody at the same time as a detached accompaniment – but now the melody is in the left hand and the accompanying chords are in the top part. Here Schumann is exploiting the warm 'tenor' register of the piano in order to create the image of the male-voiced, 'wide awake' farm-worker striding purposefully home for tea.

Warning. Photocopying any part of this book without permission is illegal.

Exploiting the Resource 45

Placing the melody in the lowest part rather than the top part is an excellent way to obtain variety when a tune is repeated – and this is just the sort of tip that you could pick up from the music you study and then put into practice in your own compositions.

Later in the piece, when Schumann repeats the opening melody, he comes up with a new texture to make the tune more forceful and to provide variety:

The melody is doubled in octaves and between these two parts the pianist must also play the accompanying chords (now thinned down a little). Schumann thoughtfully changes the phrasing for this repeat, since continuous legato is not really possible in such a busy right-hand part.

Knecht Ruprecht

This stormy piece exploits the low register of the piano to create its angry mood, before bounding upwards in great leaps. Notice how the right-hand starts low in the bass clef. The tempo indicated by the metronome mark at the start is 126 beats a minute – that's more than eight semiquavers per second! The music is punctuated by heavily accented notes (indicated v) and Schumann marks the phrase endings with three loud 'stabs', each marked *f*.

What is the cause of all this anger? If you believe the translation of the title given in many editions ('Saint Nicholas' or 'Santa Claus') you will be truly perplexed since there is not the slightest bit of yuletide spirit in this piece. So what is it about? In the traditional German version of the Father Christmas legend that Schumann knew, Santa brought presents for good children while his nasty little helper *Knecht Ruprecht* came along to beat or even carry away any children who had been bad during the previous year. This is a useful reminder that a little research on what you play can be very helpful in finding what the focus of a piece is all about – and the results may sometimes surprise you!

'Ruprecht' is a name (like Rupert); 'Knecht' means 'servant'.

Kleine Studie

46   Exploiting the Resource

In this piece Schumann exploits a device called the **broken chord** in which the notes of a chord are 'broken' (played separately but rhythmically) in ascending and descending patterns. So we have a chord of G major in bar 1 (G–B–D), a chord of C major in bar 2 (C–E–G) and so on. This is just one of a number of type of figuration – some others are shown on page 15.

Kleine Studie means 'little study' and a study is an exercise in technique. The object of this one is to develop the art of playing totally even quavers. And so Schumann continues this initial figure for the rest of the piece – 63 bars with six quavers in every one. This is a training exercise – it will not intrigue your listeners or impress your examiners! As we have indicated in previous chapters, a study is not a good type of piece to perform or use as a model for composition, since it offers too little variety.

Most studies are designed as exercises and do not make good subjects for performance to audiences or good models for composing. There are some exceptions – studies that are also great pieces of music – but they are rare and often extremely difficult!

Kleine Romanze

Here Schumann exploits the piano in yet another way – the pianist must play both melody and accompaniment in each hand simultaneously. The speed of the crotchet beat is a fraction faster than *Knecht Ruprecht*, but there are no semiquavers here so it will not seem to be so frantic.

Nevertheless, while the title tells us this is a 'little romance', the impassioned dynamics suggest that it is really a hot-blooded love affair: the music suddenly swells to *fp* (a *forte* which instantly vaporises to *piano*) and then to *sfp* – a *sforzando* (strong accent) that immediately gives way to soft tone. The passions seem to be heaving. And notice how both the treble and bass staves have the same tune – was Schumann thinking of a woman and a man singing in perfect octaves?

Gukkuk im Versteck

Our final example from the appendix to *Album for the Young* is the end of 'cuckoo in hiding'. It illustrates two points that are well worth remembering for your own compositions since they apply to all instruments and not just the piano. One is the value of unaccompanied melody, particularly in order to provide variety. The other is the importance of silence. Rests are vital and rests with pauses will really tickle the ear. They provide high contrast and they focus the mind more intently on the sounds that follow.

Warning. Photocopying any part of this book without permission is illegal.

Exploiting the Resource

Schumann's *Album for the Young* also includes pieces that use **contrapuntal** textures – in other words, music that combines two or more melodic lines. His examples are quite complicated, so here is how an older composer, J. S. Bach, exploits the ability of keyboard instruments to present two melodic parts at the same time:

Invention No. 1

J.S. Bach

This is two-part counterpoint – there is one melody in each hand. It is also imitative counterpoint, because it uses a device called **imitation** in which a melodic idea stated in one part (marked *a*) is copied in another part (*b*) while the first part continues. Can you see where imitation is used in the second bar of this example?

The music above was written in about 1723. It would have been played on the clavichord, a very quiet keyboard instrument that was popular in the home, or possibly on the harpsichord. Neither has the enormous dynamic range of the piano, which replaced both of these older instruments by the end of the 18th century. Indeed the piano's full name (*pianoforte*) means 'soft–loud' and reflects the revolutionary fact that it allowed dynamics to be varied on a note-by-note basis.

Music from the baroque period is often played on the piano nowadays, but remember that Bach was exploiting a type of keyboard instrument that had a much less resonant tone than the modern piano. Consequently pianists usually try to adopt a light touch when playing this style of music and many prefer little or no use of the sustaining pedal.

A **virtuoso** is a performer of outstanding technical brilliance.

A **concerto** is a large-scale composition for one or more solo instruments accompanied by an orchestra. It is usually in three movements.

We have explored just a few of the ways in which composers have exploited the potential of the piano – there are many more. In the 19th century, **virtuoso** pianists composed extremely difficult piano pieces that would astound audiences with the brilliance of their fingerwork. Other composers saw that the power and range of the piano made it an ideal solo instrument in the **concerto**, in which the piano could be accompanied by – and dramatically pitted against – an entire symphony orchestra.

'Harmonics' No. 102 from *Mikrokosmos*, Vol. 4

Bartók

Press down keys without sounding

Warning. Photocopying any part of this book without permission is illegal.

Some 20th-century composers exploited ways in which new types of tone colour (**timbre**) could be produced on the piano, such as the cluster chord – a very dissonant sound produced by applying the fist, forearm or a piece of wood to adjacent notes on the keyboard. A rather gentler effect is shown *left*, in which Bartók requires the left hand to hold down certain keys without playing them. This raises the dampers on these notes and allows the strings to vibrate in sympathy when notes are played by the right hand. The American composer John Cage is famous for his works for 'prepared piano' in which the performer is required to insert various objects made of metal, wood and rubber, between the strings of the piano in order to modify the timbre of certain notes.

48 Exploiting the Resource

If you are a pianist you will not be short of choice when it comes to choosing pieces to study and play, since the piano has an enormous repertoire of solo music. Finding an ensemble work that includes the piano can be more tricky since such pieces often require a pianist of quite an advanced standard. However remember that playing duets with another pianist can be hugely enjoyable. There are many original works and arrangements for piano duet (four hands on one piano). Also, if you have access to two pianos in the same room, there are many works for two pianos.

You might find a visit to www.chambermusic2000.com helpful.

If you decide to offer a piano duet for your ensemble performance it would be a good idea to team up with another pianist as soon as possible, so that you have plenty of time to get used to playing together.

We do not have the space to discuss every instrument in the same depth as the piano, but in the rest of this chapter we will draw attention to some of the issues to consider when dealing with other types of instrument.

Wind instruments

One of the most important techniques for all wind instruments is the contrast in articulation that can be achieved through the use of tongued or slurred notes, as in this example from Rossini's overture to his opera *The Thieving Magpie* (1817):

Notice how effectively the legato phrases of the oboe are answered by the cheeky staccato of the flute. Vivid contrasts of this kind can be very effective in your own compositions, so always try to work out exactly how wind music should be articulated.

When composing music for wind instruments, plan where the performers will breathe. Remember that writing music for a lone unaccompanied wind player can be especially difficult as the breathing points may be very obvious to the listener.

If you include an accompaniment or write for two or more players, it will be much easier to incorporate rests into your composition during which players will be able to take a breath. Best of all use the type of texture known as dialogue as this will provide an ample supply of natural breathing points:

Dialogue is a texture in which phrases are passed from one instrument to another.

Although we have suggested that the lower part in this example could be played on the clarinet, it could equally well be the right-hand part of a piano accompaniment to the flute. The point is that a wind player can take a breath while someone else is playing.

Remember that large instruments (and also the oboe, because it requires high breath-pressure) will need longer and more frequent rests than instruments such as the flute and recorder.

Warning. Photocopying any part of this book without permission is illegal.

Exploiting the Resource

In performance, wind players need to remember that even the most carefully-planned breathing can go wrong due to nerves. If you are anxious, breathing will always be the first thing to let you down – so remember that the more practice you get of performing to others, the less anxious you will feel. Always pay particular attention to giving final notes of phrases their full length, as these notes can often become clipped in order to snatch a breath.

Good intonation is vital for a successful performance. If you are not playing alone this means taking time to get in tune with the other instruments. Remember that you need to warm up before tuning, and check several different pitches across the range of your instrument. Accurate tuning is a skill that you should expect to spend some time practising if you are not used to playing your instrument with accompaniment. Secure pitch also means listening carefully as you play. In particular, your breath support needs to be good enough to ensure that pitch doesn't droop at the ends of long phrases. Also beware of going out of tune when playing loudly in the highest register.

As on all instruments, good tone is also important for wind players. In particular, try to avoid a thin or breathy tone. The use of vibrato is quite an advanced technique, but it can often improve woodwind tone enormously when used appropriately.

Most woodwind instruments produce very distinct tone colours in different registers. This is most obvious in the case of the clarinet, which has a wonderfully 'oily' and often sinister quality in its lowest register. The middle octave is rather more ordinary, but the top octave has a great power and brilliance.

Such vivid contrast is exploited in many works, not least in the first clarinet entry of Weber's Concerto No. 2 for clarinet and orchestra:

For maximum variety always try to exploit the available range of the instrument in your own compositions, as in this soaring flute phrase from Stephen Dodgson's *Circus-Pony*:

Remember, too, that variety can be achieved by making plenty of contrast between melodies that move by step and those that move by leap, and by using a full range of dynamics.

If you are a wind player you will know your own strengths and weaknesses, and will be able to accommodate these in your compositions. When writing for other wind players you should first discuss with them what they find easy and what may be difficult. On the next two pages we have given some basic factual information about writing for some of the more common wind instruments.

In the margin we have shown the ranges of a number of wind instruments. The white notes indicate the bottom and top pitches that can be produced by experienced players. Notes at the extremes of the range can be tricky, and it is usually better to restrict yourself to the ranges shown by the black notes when writing for players who have only been learning for a few years.

Music for the descant recorder is written an octave lower than it sounds in order to avoid using too many leger lines above the stave. Notice that the range of the treble recorder does not extend down to middle C. The recorder has a limited dynamic range – trying to perform too loudly or too quietly can easily result in sharp or flat playing. Good recorder players make up for this lack of dynamic contrast with plenty of subtle contrasts in tonguing.

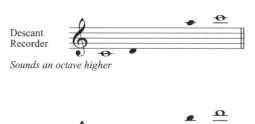
Descant Recorder
Sounds an octave higher

The bottom octave of the flute can have a beautiful tone, but it is very quiet. Many young composers make the mistake of restricting flute parts to this low register. The very pure and brilliant quality that people more commonly associate with the instrument is found in the upper register, on notes that mostly need to be written on leger lines above the stave. The sound of the flute can carry much more successfully in this upper part of its range.

Treble Recorder

The dynamic curve of the oboe is the opposite of the flute. Its lowest notes are loud, and not easy to control, while the upper octave of its range is thinner and quieter. Always remember to include plenty of long rests in oboe and bassoon parts.

Flute

The three registers of the clarinet have been mentioned above. Unlike most other wind instruments, the lowest notes are very easy to produce. Try to avoid writing clarinet parts that circle around the 'break' (between B♭ and B♮, a 7th above middle C) as this can introduce particular fingering problems.

Oboe

The most common type of clarinet is the clarinet in B♭. It is a transposing instrument, which means that its notes do not sound at their notated pitch – the clarinet in B♭ sounds a tone lower than written. Accordingly you need to write its music a tone higher than you want it to sound. For example, if you want to hear the pitches C–D–E on the clarinet in B♭, you would need to write them as D–E–F♯ in the clarinet's part.

Clarinet in B♭
Sounds a tone lower

Saxophones are also transposing instruments. The alto saxophone in E♭ sounds a major 6th lower than written while the tenor saxophone in B♭ sounds a major 9th lower. Saxophones are capable of a wide dynamic range, except on the very lowest notes, which are difficult to produce quietly.

Bassoon

Brass instruments are capable of producing a wide dynamic range, although less experienced players may find it hard to create really effective contrasts. Well-supported breathing, good tone, secure intonation and a good variety of articulation are all as important for brass players as they are for woodwind players.

Stamina can be a problem for less-experienced players, so include plenty of rests in your compositions to allow the lip to recover.

Saxophone
Alto saxophone sounds a major 6th lower
Tenor saxophone sounds a major 9th lower

Producing the required pitch for a note on a brass instrument is not just a question of pressing the correct valves or finding the right

Warning. Photocopying any part of this book without permission is illegal.

Exploiting the Resource 51

position for the slide on a trombone. It also requires exactly the correct lip tension when buzzing the lips to produce a note. This can be quite difficult for less-experienced players, but there are several things that composers can do to help.

Firstly, it may be better to avoid the type of triadic writing that is associated with brass fanfares. Slow melodies that move by step are often much easier. Remember that long notes can be very effective when held against a more rhythmic accompaniment. In particular, sustained notes with changing dynamics offer a good opportunity to exploit the instrument's beauty of tone, as in this modern Pavan for horn and piano by Stephen Dodgson:

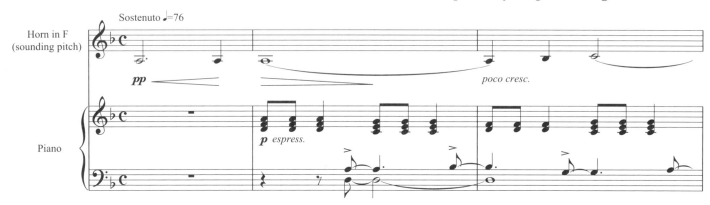

Secondly, try to include some pitch 'signposts' in your brass parts. For instance it will help novice brass players if their first note is the same pitch as the last note of an introduction played on the piano. Or you could ensure that the brass player's second phrase begins on the same pitch as the last note of their first phrase. This sort of attention to detail can help performers get off to a much more confident start.

Brass instruments generally have a narrower range than woodwind instruments and there is less opportunity to exploit contrasts between different registers. However they are capable of a wide range of articulation, from the gentlest legato to the most explosive attack.

It is also possible to modify the tone of a brass instrument by using a mute. In its simplest form this is a conical object that is wedged inside the bell of the instrument to make the tone thinner and quieter. The result is often a bit like an echo effect.

Trumpet and trombone players in jazz, film and light music often need a wide range of different mutes, such as the 'wah-wah' and 'harmon' mutes much over-used for comic effects on cartoon soundtracks.

If you need to use a mute in a brass composition, remember that the player will need adequate time in which to insert and remove the device. Mutes often badly affect the pitch of the instrument and players need to know how to compensate for this, so it is best not to depend on the use of a mute unless you are writing for an experienced brass player.

The horn is played with the right hand just inside the bell of the instrument. This warms the tone and also allows fine control over pitch while playing. If the right hand is held in a closed position and moved further inside the bell the air flow is restricted and a

Warning. Photocopying any part of this book without permission is illegal.

52   Exploiting the Resource

muted effect is produced. This is called hand stopping, and is often indicated by a '+' sign over the notes affected. When played very loudly, this can cause the horn's tone to become menacingly strident – it is an effect beloved of composers who write music for horror films!

Horn in F

Sounds a perfect 5th lower

The horn in F is a transposing instrument that sounds a perfect 5th lower than written. Parts for the horn in F should normally be written in the treble clef, a perfect 5th higher than you wish them to sound.

Trumpet in B♭

Sounds a tone lower

The most common type of trumpet today is the trumpet in B♭. It is a transposing instrument that, like the clarinet in B♭, sounds a tone lower than written. Parts for the trumpet in B♭ therefore need to be written a tone higher than you wish them to sound.

Trombone

In classical music the trombone is usually notated in the bass clef (with any really high parts in the tenor clef) and is not treated as a transposing instrument.

Tuba

There are several different sizes of tuba, of which the tuba in F (whose range is shown *right*) is just one. Again, in classical music the tuba is not treated as a transposing instrument and is normally notated only in the bass clef.

However in the brass-band tradition even bass instruments are sometimes notated in the treble clef and treated as transposing instruments. So, for instance, the trombone may be written in the treble clef and treated as a transposing instrument in B♭, for which the notes will sound a major 9th lower than written. You will need to check these more complicated requirements carefully with your performers and teacher.

Strings

The strings are among the most versatile of all instruments. They offer a wide pitch range, a full dynamic range and many different shades of tone colour. Also, unlike notes played on wind instruments and the piano, bowed notes can be sustained indefinitely.

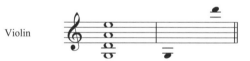

Violin

The staves in the margin show the pitches of the four strings on each instrument, followed by the range that a player who has been learning for about three years is likely to be able to manage. Experienced players will be able to reach top notes that are very much higher than the ones shown here.

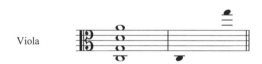

Viola

Music for the violin is always written in the treble clef. Viola parts are normally written in the alto clef (see page 6) although the treble clef is used for higher notes. Cello parts are written in the bass clef, although more experienced players will learn to read the tenor and treble clefs for high notes.

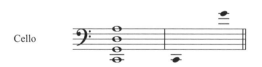

Cello

The double bass normally uses the bass clef and it sounds an octave lower than written. Again, other clefs are sometimes used for the highest notes. Notice that the double bass (like the bass guitar) has strings that are tuned a 4th apart, while the other three string instruments have strings that are tune in 5ths. Also note that the lowest note on many double basses is E, although instruments that extend down to low C are also found.

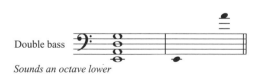

Double bass

Sounds an octave lower

Exploiting the Resource 53

Each string has its own distinctive tone colour, the lowest being the warmest and the highest being the brightest. We can see how Elgar exploits this in the following beautiful melody which gets louder and brighter as it crosses the four strings of the violin:

The direction, speed, position, angle and weight of the bow stroke are all crucial in producing good tone and in achieving variety of attack and dynamic. A down bow (indicated ⊓) generally creates a firmer, more incisive attack than an up bow (indicated V). Legato playing needs smooth changes in bow direction. Staccato can be very effective on string instruments, and more advanced players learn a variety of bow strokes to achieve different effects, such as the light, bouncing stroke known as *spiccato*.

Bowing nearer to the bridge (*sul ponticello*) can produce a thin, eerie sound, while a less sonorous tone is produced by bowing over the fingerboard (*sul tasto*). In order to produce a powerful and deliberately crude tone the hair near the heel of the bow is used (usually indicated by the French term *au talon*).

Very rapid up- and down-bows on a single pitch or chord result in a dramatic rustling effect known as a bowed **tremolo**. A fingered tremolo (the rapid alternation of two notes a 3rd or more apart) is played on one string in the same way as a trill.

All string instruments can produce a rich, warm tone when *vibrato* is used. This undulating sound is produced by a rocking motion of the left hand that causes a wavering of the pitch of a note. It is so common that most experienced players use it unless instructed not to do so. However vibrato is often not taught in the early years of string playing, so less experienced players may not use it.

Various special effects are available on string instruments. They may be plucked (**pizzicato**) instead of bowed (**arco**). Remember that less experienced players will need a few seconds to adjust from playing with the bow to using pizzicato and vice versa.

Mutes, which clip on to the bridge and thus dampen its vibrations, reduce the volume and change the tone colour to a more veiled sound. The instruction *con sordino* means 'with mute' and the words *senza sordino* are used when the mute is to be removed. Again, remember that players need a rest of a few seconds in order to apply or remove a mute.

More advanced effects include touching the string lightly (instead of pressing it against the fingerboard) in order to produce a pure, flute-like sound known as a harmonic. Sliding the finger up or down a string while bowing it causes the pitch to glide from one note to another in a *glissando*. The effect known as *col legno* (with the wood) is produced by reversing the bow and bouncing it on the strings. Real pitches can be heard, but they are accompanied by brittle percussive sounds. It is an effect that works best when used by a whole section of strings (as in 'Mars' from Holst's *Planets* suite) rather than by a solo instrument.

String players (and singers) often use the term **portamento** to describe a continuous glide of pitch from one note to another.

Warning. Photocopying any part of this book without permission is illegal.

Singing

For singers the 'resource' of the human voice is very personal and individual. Songs need to be projected effectively, and this includes conveying the meaning of the words as well as the music. Consonants need to be crisp and clear, but they should not impede the flow of vowel sounds, since it is the latter that carry the musical line. Breathing needs to be well supported so that the music doesn't fade away or fall in pitch at the ends of phrases. Take special care to ensure that the final notes of phrases are not clipped.

Consider exactly how the voice is used in different types of vocal music. Some songs include rapid patter, with many repeated pitches, in order to convey a large amount of information quickly. Some, such as Gershwin's famous *Summertime* are based on relatively short, falling phrases: 'Summertime ... an' the livin' is easy ... Fish are jumpin' ... an' the cotton is high'. Other songs are based on long phrases with elegant arching lines:

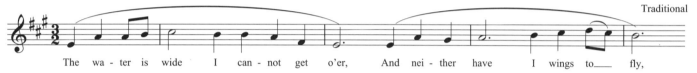

The style of word-setting in this example is known as syllabic – with the exception of the word 'to' there is one note per syllable. Vocal music in which many notes have to be sung to a single syllable is known as melismatic:

Melodic movement by step is often associated with vocal music, but see how leaps are exploited for expressive effect and note especially how climactic high notes are treated. When writing your own songs it will make the singer's task easier if you can arrange for high notes to be set to open vowel sounds such as 'ah', rather than to awkward dipthongs such as 'may'.

As in all types of performance, try to establish the character of the music. What is it that you are trying to convey to the listener? Some songs require the singer to take on the role of an actor, others require the singer to be a narrator. In some songs the singer may even have to portray several different characters.

Whatever your instrument, decide on the key elements you wish to communicate in your performance: rhythmic drive, a dreamy atmosphere, elegant phrasing, dramatic contrasts or subtle blends. Look for clues in the title, the performing directions and the way the instrument is exploited.

Then focus in on the fine detail. Rather than just deciding that a piece should sound 'happy', work out whether you want it to sound witty, boisterous, contented, frivolous, celebratory, cheeky or merely cheerful. If it is 'sad', try to focus on whether you mean tragic, doom-laden, nostalgic, angry or solemn. Approach composing in the same way, making sure that you fully exploit the resources of the instrument in order to achieve your aim.

Warning. Photocopying any part of this book without permission is illegal.

Techniques of Melodic Composition

You need to study techniques of melody writing because you will have to create a melody for the Terminal Task (see page 37) and there will also be questions on melodies in the listening paper. In this chapter we will concentrate especially on the types of melody you may encounter in that paper.

Plainchant

Plainchant (or plainsong) was traditionally sung in services of the Roman Catholic church. It consists of an unaccompanied melody – this is known as a **monophonic** musical texture. Plainsong was intended to be sung in the resonant acoustics of a large, stone-built church. Example 1 shows a plainsong melody that is a hymn about the Holy Spirit and is at least 1,000 years old.

Example 1   An ancient plainsong hymn from the Vatican library

Do you notice anything odd about the way it is written? It's not so much what is there as what is not there: no stems or tails to the note heads (and therefore no indication of rhythm) and no time signature or proper barlines (and therefore no regular pulse or metre). Of course you can't sing the hymn without rhythm – in fact music cannot exist without rhythm. But if you listen to a recording of a plainsong melody it will almost certainly be sung in a flowing manner with no underlying beat or metre.

Now play, or better still, sing the melody. Did you feel that the fourth phrase and the Amen ended on the wrong note? Would the melody have sounded more complete if it had the alternative ending we have composed for it? If your answer to both questions is yes this is because we are all surrounded by **tonal music** (music in major or minor keys). On the radio, on television, in films – everywhere we hear music that doesn't sound complete until it ends on the tonic. In fact Example 1 contains all of the pitches of the scale of C major, but notice that the hymn begins and ends on G, and the tune revolves around this pitch in the first and last phrases and in the Amen.

The melody of Example 1 is based on a **modal** scale called the mixolydian mode (see page 12). Because tunes based on this mode finish on G this pitch is called the final wherever it occurs. The pitch that gives the end of the hymn such a strong modal flavour is the F♮, the seventh degree of the modal scale. It lies a whole tone below the final note (G), unlike the leading note of G major (F♯) which is just a semitone below the tonic. More than any other degree of the scale it is the use of this note that gives a modal feel to most plainsong and many folk melodies.

You might have noticed how the plainsong melody revolves round C in phrases 2 and 3 in much the same way as phrases 1 and 4 revolve around G. This gives shape to the melody. All four phrases are linked by the way they circle around G or C, but phrases 1 and 4 are at a lower pitch level (reaching down to F) than phrases 2 and 3 (which reach up to E).

Notice that most of the melody moves by step. There are leaps of up to a perfect 5th but there are never two leaps together. This helps to maintain the flowing feel of the whole melody. Finally notice that the melody all falls within a range of a 7th (F–E).

Test yourself

1. What is the final of a mode?
   ....

2. Define 'monophonic'
   ....

3. Where might you expect to hear plainchant sung?
   ....

Composing

Using the English translation of Example 1 (made by the English poet, Robert Bridges) compose your own plainsong melody in the dorian mode (D–E–F–G–A–B–C–D). You might find it easier to make a convincing final cadence if you also use the C below this scale, but keep within an octave, use mostly stepwise movement, and try to give shape to your melody by using some of the techniques we have already discussed.

Folk music of the British Isles

Folk music is an oral tradition, meaning that over the years the music has been handed down from generation to generation without being written down, causing the music to vary over time and to be interpreted differently by individual musicians. This often leads to regional variations – i.e the same song may sound totally different when performed by musicians in different parts of the country. Folk music exists in many different forms, from music for dancing (such as jigs and reels) to industrial songs, love ballads and songs that tell a legend or a story.

Many folk melodies are based on a scale of five pitches known as a **pentatonic** scale (see page 11). Example 2 (on page 58) is a major pentatonic melody starting on G. It sounds like G major because so many phrases begin and end on G and because the four bars with brackets above them are made from the tonic chord of G major:

In this context folk means 'of the people'.

Try whispering a very short poem to a class mate, then pass it on from person to person until everyone has heard it. You will probably be quite surprised by how different your original poem is from the version that the last person hears.

Warning. Photocopying any part of this book without permission is illegal.

Techniques of Melodic Composition

Example 2 The Green Bushes

So in spite of the fact that the pitches C and F♯ are not used we would be justified in saying that this tune is in G major. Like many simple melodies *The Green Bushes* is made up of four four-bar phrases. Some melodies begin on a strong beat, but, like many other folk songs, Example 2 begins on a weak beat. Each phrase of *The Green Bushes* begins with an anacrusis or upbeat (see page 16) and is 12 beats (the equivalent of four bars) in length. The phrases are printed on separate staves to make this clear.

Let's look at the form of *The Green Bushes*. The first and last phrases are virtually the same, and they both end on the tonic of G major, so we will call them both A. Both the second and third phrases end on the supertonic (the second degree of the scale of G major), but there is an important difference between them which is why we identify the third phrase as B¹ not B. Where the second phrase ends with repeated notes, the third phrase swoops up a 6th to form a climax on the word 'sweetly' before falling to the supertonic. Like most folk songs *The Green Bushes* is **strophic**. This means that it has the same melody for every verse of the **lyrics**.

In contrast to the pastoral nature of *The Green Bushes* is *Poverty Knock*, an industrial folksong of the late 19th century that laments a factory weaver's life. Despite the harsh nature of the lyrics, the melody is in a major key with regular phrases that usually end either on the tonic or the dominant. Listen to *Poverty Knock* – do you think that the rhythmic nature of the recurring line in the chorus ('poverty, poverty knock') could be said to imitate the sound of the weaver's loom?

Poverty Knock is discussed in *Aural Matters* (Bowman and Terry, Schott 1993) alongside a recording of the piece.

Test yourself

1. What is meant by a melody that moves by step?
   ....

2. Add the name of the next note in this major pentatonic scale of D: D–E–F♯–A– ......

3. The aeolian mode is based on the scale A–B–C–D–E–F–G–A. Which of these notes is the final of the aeolian mode? ......

4. What is an anacrusis?
   ....

Warning. Photocopying any part of this book without permission is illegal.

58   Techniques of Melodic Composition

Composing

Compose your own pentatonic song with the ABB[1]A form of *The Green Bushes* using this verse of the lyrics:

> Come let us be going kind sir if you please
> Come let us be going from under these trees
> For yonder is coming my true love I see
> Down by the green bushes where he thinks to meet me.

Melody in the baroque and classical periods

By the end of the 17th century the last traces of modality had virtually disappeared and the major/minor system of tonality reigned supreme. In modal melodies variety could be achieved by ending phrases on different degrees of the mode. In Example 1, for instance, the four phrases end on the fourth, fifth, fourth and final of the mode. In tonal music it became possible to modulate from the original key to a new key by cancelling out one or more of the pitches of the old key and replacing them with one or more pitches belonging to a new key. This happens at the end of the first stave of Example 3.

Keys and modulation

Example 3   Handel, Air *The Harmonious Blacksmith* from Keyboard Suite in E (original key E major)

The melody begins in the tonic key of F major. But at the end of the first stave B♭ rises to C causing a modulation which takes the melody to the dominant key of C major. In the original keyboard version the modulation is even clearer because this ending is harmonised with the dominant and tonic chords of the new key, creating a perfect cadence. So it is natural that Handel should reinforce the cadence at the end of the Air with chords V and I, which make another perfect cadence, this time back in the tonic key of F major.

Binary form

Form in music is the shape that patterns of notes make as they unfold through time. This is a bit like structure in architecture, which is the shape that buildings make in space.

Composers soon realised that the use of contrasting keys could help structure a melody. Play or sing Example 3 without repeats and without harmony. Do you agree that the modulation to C major marks the end of a section of the piece, but that it doesn't sound like the end? It needs another section to make complete musical sense. This type of form is known as **binary** form because it has two sections (A and B in Example 3), both of them ending with clear cadences. When the melody is played with repeats the true form is AABB, but it is still called binary form.

> **Warning.** Photocopying any part of this book without permission is illegal.

You can also hear many binary-form dances in baroque suites such as Handel's *Fireworks Music* and *Water Music*, and Bach's four orchestral suites. Most music departments will have CDs of these works.

Most baroque dances are in binary form – look out for minuets, gavottes, bourrées, sarabandes and gigues by composers such as Corelli, Handel and Bach. Such dances are often used as teaching pieces so see how many students in your group can perform one such movement to the class. The rest of you should try to identify the key (eg tonic, dominant, relative major) and type of cadence (perfect or imperfect) used at the end of the A section.

Variations

Repetition and varied repetition were important techniques that ensured both unity and variety in the melodies that are typical of the late baroque and classical periods. They were often based on the smallest melodic unit – the motif. Complete melodies are often created by repeating and varying a few related motifs. For instance, look at the melody in Example 3. It starts with a pair of quavers forming a rising 3rd. Can you see how this motif recurs throughout the melody? First it is augmented (enlarged) to a rising 4th and then, at the end of bar 2, it is augmented again to a rising 6th. In the B section the rising interval has been inverted, becoming a falling 2nd (D–C in bars 3–4) and a falling 5th (C–F in bars 5–6).

Another important motif is the one we have marked with a bracket. Can you see how this too is used in many different permutations in the rest of the melody? All of this must seem about as musical as algebra – but can you hear how Handel has spun out the simplest possible idea (two quavers) in such a way that they provide both unity and variety to the whole melody?

Handel wrote five variations on the tune printed in Example 3. Here is the start of the first variation, printed below the notes of the original theme:

This is one of the simplest types of variation, and was known in the baroque era by the French term *double*. If you compare the two staves above you will see that Handel adds enough extra notes between each of the original notes to make continuous semiquaver figuration. In this way he virtually doubles the number of notes – hence the French term!

Ask your teacher to play the variations and you will hear that in the second the semiquavers are in the bass, and that in the third and fourth variations the melody is disguised amid semiquaver triplets. In the last variation, and with a great show of bravado, the original melody is submerged in a welter of demisemiquavers. The openings of these variations are printed *left*.

Most music departments will have recordings of the works listed in the margin of page 61 – they all include examples of variation form from the classical period (approximately 1750–1825). As you listen try to identify how each variation relates to the theme. Many variations are created by using one or more of the following techniques:

Warning. Photocopying any part of this book without permission is illegal.

60 Techniques of Melodic Composition

- ✦ Adding extra notes to decorate the theme
- ✦ Removing notes to reduce the theme to a skeleton
- ✦ Adding one or more additional melodies to the theme
- ✦ Changing the chords used to harmonise the theme
- ✦ Using the original chords but substituting a new tune
- ✦ Changing the key from major to minor (or vice versa)
- ✦ Changing the metre
- ✦ Adding a persistent accompaniment figure (such as a triplet pattern or march rhythm), sometimes done in order to give a variation a particular character.

Haydn: second movement of the 'Emperor' Quartet, Op. 76 No. 3; Mozart: fourth movement of the Clarinet Quintet, K581; Schubert: fourth movement of 'The Trout' Quintet, Op. 114. Also look out for Mozart's 12 Variations on *Ah, vous dirai-je, Maman* (which is the tune also known as *Twinkle, twinkle little star*) and Beethoven's seven variations on *God Save the King*. Both of these works are for piano.

Ternary form

Throughout the 18th century the most popular dance was the stately triple-time minuet. It was often paired with a second minuet that became known as a trio. At the end of the trio the instruction *Menuet da capo* (sometimes abbreviated to Men. D.C.) indicates that the minuet should be repeated. In this way what we hear is a three-section structure called ternary form (minuet–trio–minuet).

Minuet is often spelled *menuet* or *minuetto*.

The term trio arose because originally this contrasting minuet was written in three-part harmony, often for a trio of instruments.

Example 4   Haydn, Minuet and Trio from Keyboard Sonata in C, Hob. XVI/7

Ask your teacher to play Example 4 with the repeat of the minuet after the trio. It's very easy to hear the ternary structure in this movement because the minuet is in C major and the trio is in the strongly contrasting key of C minor.

There are some compositional devices to notice in this piece. Can you see that in bars 1–2 the four notes labelled 'a' are immediately repeated a step lower (b)? This is called a **sequence**. There is another sequence in bars 25–28, but this time d is one step higher than c. Now compare x in the first stave with x¹ in the second stave. Can you see that x¹ is exactly the same as x except that it is a 5th lower?

Warning. Photocopying any part of this book without permission is illegal.

Techniques of Melodic Composition   **61**

Church organists often transpose hymn tunes to a lower pitch so that all members of the congregation can sing the high notes.

This is not a sequence because the second phrase does not immediately follow the first phrase. When a passage is repeated at a different pitch some time after the original passage the music is said to be **transposed**. The same term applies to the performance of a whole piece at a different pitch to the printed pitch. Finally notice that the rhythm as well as the key of the trio contrasts with the minuet. Whereas all phrases of the minuet are on the beat, most bars of the melody of the trio are syncopated. Compare bar 1 with bar 17. In bar 1 there is a note on every crotchet beat, whereas in bar 17 every melody note is off the beat.

Many longer pieces of late 18th-century instrumental music contain a minuet and trio as one of the movements. Such pieces include symphonies, chamber music (for small groups such as string quartets) and sonatas for one or two instruments.

Rondo form

A recording of this rondo is included in *Aural Matters in Practice* by David Bowman and Paul Terry (Schott, 1994).

A rondo is a movement in which a melody called the **refrain** alternates with contrasting melodies called **episodes** to form a pattern such as ABACA:

Example 5 Henry Purcell, Rondeau from *Abdelazar* (1695)

Warning. Photocopying any part of this book without permission is illegal.

62 Techniques of Melodic Composition

Purcell creates a bold opening by starting his melody with a rising arpeggio on the tonic chord of D minor. This is balanced by stepwise movement (bar 2) that features **passing notes**. These are notes that fill the gaps between harmony notes – they are marked * in the example *right*. Now look at the melody in bar 3 – does it move by step or by leap? And how does Purcell use this melodic figure in bars 4–6?

The melody of the first episode (B) starts with a transposed version of the first two bars of the refrain. In what key is episode B?

Episode C contrasts with earlier material in rhythm (it introduces dotted patterns) and in key – it starts in A minor and then modulates back to the tonic (D minor), ending with an imperfect cadence. Notice that Purcell makes extensive use of sequences in all three sections of the work.

By the end of the 18th century composers had developed the rondo into the type of substantial but jolly movement that you can hear as the finale of works such as Haydn's Trumpet Concerto in E♭.

The refrain of this rondo forms the theme of a set of variations by the 20th-century composer Benjamin Britten, in his *Young Person's Guide to the Orchestra*. Try to listen to this work, and compare it with Purcell's original rondo, as it will introduce you to many different kinds of variation technique and instrumental writing.

This work is available on *Britten – Orchestral Works*, Apex (8573 89082-2).

Test yourself

1. If a musical form is described as ABA[1]:

    (a) What does the small figure [1] indicate?

    ....

    (b) What technical term describes this musical structure?

    ....

2. At the start of Example 3 the opening interval of a rising 3rd is melodically augmented. What does augmented mean in this context?

    ....

3. In what form is the minuet section of Example 4?

    ....

4. What are the most important differences between the minuet and the trio in Example 4?

    ....

    ....

5. In a rondo form such as ABACABA, sections B and C are known as episodes. What is the correct term for section A?

    ....

Composing

Either choose a short tune that you like, or compose one, and then write at least two variations on it. There is no need to imitate a classical style in your work – you could, for instance, compose variations on 'Happy birthday to you' in two or more modern dance styles. Use some of the techniques listed above in your variations.

Warning. Photocopying any part of this book without permission is illegal.

Techniques of Melodic Composition 63

20th-century innovations

Serialism

The word chromatic comes from the ancient Greek for 'colour'.

In much 19th-century music chromatic notes were used to add colour to the ordinary scale notes (called diatonic notes). By the beginning of the 20th century some composers were using so many chromatic notes that they were not just colouring the tonality, they were swamping it. The music that Schoenberg (1874–1951) composed at the start of the century was like this – so full of chromatic colour that it was often difficult to know what key it was in (if any). If there are so many chromatic notes that you can't detect a key at all the music becomes **atonal**, and if it's atonal it becomes difficult to compose long movements that have clearly defined form. Schoenberg was a revolutionary who was not going to go back to the old tonal system, but he realised that a new method of composition would have to be developed to give shape or form to atonal music. The answer was to accept the chromatic scale as the basis for composition. To give structure to the music as well as to make sure that there were no remnants of tonality, the 12 chromatic tones would be arranged in a particular order called a series (or tone row), and theoretically no single pitch could be repeated until all 12 had been used.

In a sense all **serial music** is a continuous set of variations on a theme because it consists of various permutations of the pitches in the original series. Webern was a pupil of Schoenberg and the music shown in Example 6 is typical of his style.

Example 6 Webern, extracts from Piano Variations, Op. 27

Pitch classes are pitches with the same letter names.

Pointillism is a term borrowed from art where it refers to those impressionist paintings that are made from thousands of tiny dots of paint.

Warning. Photocopying any part of this book without permission is illegal.

The theme of these variations is a tone row consisting of the pitches E♭–B♮–B♭–D♮–C♯–C♮–F♯–E♮–G♮–F♮–A♮–G♯. This original order of the tone row is called the **prime order** or basic series. You can see in Example 6a that Webern has laid out these 12 pitch classes with huge leaps and complicated rhythms. The spiky result sounds like random dots of sound, which can be described as pointillist. There are several ways in which the prime order itself can be manipulated. The easiest to understand is the **retrograde order** in which the row is played backwards (Example 6b). Notice that when Webern uses this variant of the row he compresses it so that notes 4 and 5 sound simultaneously (a process called verticalisation).

64 Techniques of Melodic Composition

There are almost as many melodic styles in serial music as there are in tonal music, as a comparison of Webern's spiky pointillism with Berg's evenly flowing violin ascent (Example 7) suggests.

Example 7 Berg, Violin Concerto, prime order at bar 15 of the first movement

Notice that Berg has made three quarters of his row out of overlapping major and minor triads, so if the notes are telescoped in a similar manner to the way Webern compressed his row, we are likely to finish up with concords or complete triads. So the series of pitches a composer chooses for his prime order can affect the whole composition, not just its melodic lines.

There are two other orders for the note row in serial music. One is the **inversion**, which you can find by counting the number of semitones between each pair of notes in the prime order and then moving the same number of semitones in the opposite direction. The example *right* shows the inverted pitches of Berg's note row from Example 7. The final order, **retrograde inversion**, is produced by playing this inverted row backwards.

Any of the pitches within the four basic orders (prime, retrograde, inversion and retrograde inversion) can be freely distributed across different octaves and all four basic orders can be transposed so they start on any of the 12 degrees of a chromatic scale.

In Example 7, how many semitones are there between each of the last four notes? Although the notation is complicated, each of these notes are two semitones (one whole tone) apart. They held a particular significance for Berg because they appeared at the start of one of Bach's chorale harmonisations, the whole of which Berg quotes in the last movement of his concerto. A whole-tone scale (eg C–D–E–F♯–G♯–A♯–C) is as atonal as the chromatic scale. Improvise with these pitches and you will immediately discover that unless you repeat one pitch far more often than any other your melody will just drift along in a tonal haze. This is precisely what Debussy wanted for his piano prelude entitled *Voiles*. The title itself is hazy: it is French for 'veils' or 'sails', and Debussy, probably deliberately, never explained the meaning of his mysterious title. In fact both words fit. The tonality is veiled but the whole-tone harmonies (mostly atonal augmented chords like those shown in Example 8a overleaf) seem to shimmer like the reflections of sails in the water on a hot summer's day.

The whole-tone scale

Voiles is available on *Piano Works Vol 4* (Naxos, 8553293).

Warning. Photocopying any part of this book without permission is illegal.

Techniques of Melodic Composition **65**

Example 8 Extracts from Debussy's *Voiles*

(a) bars 15–16

(b) bars 63–64

whole-tone scale

The only hint of a tonal anchor for these sails is the repeated bass B♭ that is heard throughout most of the prelude. This **pedal** makes us think that the prelude might end on a chord of B♭ major. But no, the tonality remains veiled until the very end where an ascending form of the whole-tone scale that has been used throughout all but a few bars of the prelude leads, not to B♭, but to the interval of a 3rd on middle C (Example 8b).

Test yourself

1. What is atonal music?
   ....

2. What is meant by the retrograde version of a tone row?
   ....

3. What are the next two pitches in the following whole-tone scale?

   D♭ – E♭ – F – G – ...... – ......

Composing

1. Write a short serial composition for unaccompanied instrument or voice based on the tone row C, B, D, C♯, E, E♭, F♯, F♮, A♭, G, B♭, A♮. Work out the retrograde version of this row, the inverted version and the retrograde inversion. Your piece should open with a statement of the note row in its prime order (remember that you can write each pitch class in any octave), and then it is up to you to decide which version of the row to use next. Try to make your composition 8–16 bars long, and keep the rhythm fairly simple.

   Note that it is unusual to find all four basic orders in a short piece. Also remember that serialism is not about using maths to create music. Serial pieces may be very concentrated and dissonant, but they should have melodic shape, interplay of ideas, variety of texture with clear points of tension and repose, a sense of style, and idiomatic instrumental writing.

2. Compose a dreamy prelude in ternary form that uses the

whole-tone scale in the A sections and the pentatonic scale in the B section.

The blues

The origins of the blues can be traced to the music of Africa, whose traditions came to the southern USA with the slave trade. Early blues songs were often about the miserable life endured by slaves (and former slaves) and the African influences on the music include the use of:

✦ Call and response

✦ Swung and syncopated rhythms

✦ Blue notes.

Let's look at each of these in turn. **Call and response** refers to a style of performing in which a soloist presents a phrase which is then answered (often echoed or varied) by a group of musicians.

Swung rhythm refers to a style of performing in which the beat is divided into pairs of notes of unequal length, the first being roughly twice the length of the second. So the pattern shown in (a) below – which we could call a straight rhythm – will be performed approximately as shown in (b) if the rhythm is swung.

Swung rhythm is common not only in the blues but also in some kinds of pop music and many kinds of jazz.

Syncopation occurs when a note on a strong beat is anticipated (ie sounded early so that it occurs on a weak beat). If we combine syncopation with swung rhythm, the phrase printed at (a) above may well be performed as shown at (d) below by a blues singer:

Blue notes can be traced back to traditional African singing, in which certain pitches are sung slightly flat in comparison to western scales. Sometimes these pitches were approached by a glide into the note (a technique we now call pitch bending) to give expressive effect to the words. The notes that were sung flat were usually the third and seventh degrees of the scale. These (and sometimes the flat fifth as well) became the standard blue notes in jazz music. The 'blues scale' can take several different forms, of which the one shown *right* is among the most common.

In the 1920s the blues style became known to a wider audience through the recordings of singers such as Ma Rainey and Bessie Smith. It was at about this time that the **12-bar blues** emerged as the predominant form. This consists of a structure based on the three primary triads (chords I, IV and V) which are played in a 12-bar pattern that is repeated throughout most or all of the piece:

| I | I | I | I | IV | IV | I | I | V | IV | I | I |

The 12 bars are generally divided into three phrases of four bars each, as shown above. The chord pattern is repeated a number of times (once for each verse in a traditional blues song), and it supports melodic lines that are often at least partly improvised. There may also be other sections (such as an introduction, a coda and bridge passages) that do not use the main chord pattern.

Rhythm

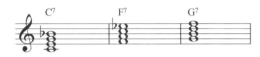

There are many versions of the basic chord pattern, including some extended to 16 bars. One of the most common variants is to add a minor 7th to some or all of the chords. In C major these chords would be C^7, F^7 and G^7 (see *left*).

Test yourself

1. Name three features of African music often heard in the blues.

   ....

   ....

   ....

2. Write out the names of the notes in chords I^7, IV^7 and V^7 in the key of G major:

   ....

3. Here is a 12-bar blues pattern in D major. Complete the missing chord symbols:

   D – D – D – D   ...... – ...... – D – D   ...... – ...... – D – D

Composing

Compose a blues melody in C using the 12-bar blues chord sequence and the blues scale. The melody should be 24 bars long and should consist of short, rhythmic phrases which emphasise some of the blue notes of the scale. Here is a possible starting point for you:

The effect of a blue note is often simulated on a keyboard instrument by playing normal and flattened versions of the note simultaneously or near-simultaneously.

Indian classical music

Indian classical music was originally perceived as an art form for the educated. Traditional performances are often given to a knowledgeable audience, where most listeners understand the parameters set by the melodic and rhythmic framework. The music is based around improvisation, although short, fixed compositions are often juxtaposed with this.

Melody   Melodic improvisation in Indian music is based upon a set collection of ascending and descending notes. This is called a **rāg**, and is

68   Techniques of Melodic Composition

somewhere between a melody and a scale in function. See the example on page 70.

Quite often the ascending and descending forms of the rāg are different. In the unfolding of a melodic improvisation, certain pitches within the rāg will be embellished, some will just be hinted at, and sometimes it is required that particular pitches are played slightly sharp or flat. Special melodic phrases are also characteristic of each rāg.

You may encounter different spellings of rāg, such as raga or ragam.

Rhythm

The basis for rhythmic improvisation is a cycle of beats called a tāl. The tāl is divided into a fixed number of beats (*matras*) and is distinguished by how these are grouped together. The basic framework of tāls can be demonstrated using a system of counting and clapping. Here is the ten-beat *jhaptal* cycle:

count	**1**	2	**3**	4	5	**6**	7	**8**	9	10
clap	×		×			O		×		

'O' signifies a weaker beat, and is often indicated simply by a hand gesture in the air.

Form

A typical rāg performance will have the following structure:

Alap	Jhor	Jhala	Gat/Bandish
Opening improvisatory section. Notes of the rāg will be introduced by the soloist. Unaccompanied, unmetred and in slow tempo.	Structured improvisatory section with a sense of metre. Medium tempo.	Music becomes faster and more rhythmic. Often colourful instrumental/vocal techniques are used.	Set composition, either vocal (*bandish*) or instrumental (*gat*) that uses the notes of the rāg. The section in which percussion will enter.

Instruments

The two instruments most commonly associated with north Indian classical music are the sitar and tabla. The **sitar** is a long-necked plucked string instrument with a gourd resonator at its lower end. Many sitars also have an extra gourd resonator at the top of the neck. The instrument has moveable frets and six or seven main strings, four of which are used for the melody and the other two or three supply a drone. Twelve or more sympathetic strings sound in response to melody notes as they are played, giving the sitar its distinctive shimmering sound.

Sitar

The **tabla** is a pair of single-headed drums. The smaller drum (*tabla*) is usually wooden and barrel-shaped and the larger, lower-pitched drum (*baya*) is made of metal and is bowl-shaped. The tabla are played with the hands, and many different sounds can be produced by a variety of finger strokes and patterns.

Tabla

Test yourself

1. What is a rāg?

   ....

2. What happens in an *alap* section?

   ....

Composing

The following rāg is called *darbari kanada*. It has a set ascending and descending pattern of notes – the ascending pattern simply moves upwards by step, but the descending pattern has more melodic interest as it is divided into two, clear phrases.

Warning. Photocopying any part of this book without permission is illegal.

Techniques of Melodic Composition **69**

Darbari kanada

Darbari kanada is a rāg that is traditionally played in the evening. Try to make your composition reflect the sultry, calm, reflective atmosphere of an Indian summer's evening.

A characteristic feature of rāg *darbari kanada* is that the third note (in this case E♭) is played or sung very flat and is always embellished with a slow trill.

Using the notes and in-built melodic phrases of *darbari kanada* compose a short piece for an unaccompanied solo instrument or voice. Divide your piece into three sections, each about 20 seconds long. The first section should be slow and unmetred and you should focus this around the shape of the rāg. The second section should be slightly faster and metrical, and should introduce a short melodic idea. The third section should be in a fast tempo with a clear sense of beat, and the melodic idea should be developed (perhaps by adding some extra embellishment, by playing or singing in a higher octave and so on).

Warning. Photocopying any part of this book without permission is illegal.

Techniques of Melodic Composition

Listening tests

1. Listen to the first 20 seconds of track 1 on Naxos CD 8.550711 THREE times before answering the following questions. The words, which are in Latin, are...
   Adorate Deum omnes Angeli ejus
   They mean...
   Adore God, all you his angels.

   (a) Underline the vocal resources used in this extract:

   Solo voice   Many voices in unison

   Many voices in octaves   Many voices in harmony

   (b) How would you describe the texture of the opening music? Select one of the following:

   Contrapuntal   Monophonic   Homophonic

   (c) In what sort of building would this music normally be sung? ....

   (d) What type of scale is the melody based on? Select one of the following:

   Major   Minor   Whole tone   Modal

2. Listen to the first 54 seconds of the fourth movement of Schubert's *Trout* Quintet (available on Telarc CD80225). Listen to this extract FOUR times before answering the following questions:

   Here is the rhythm of the first phrase of the melody:

   (a) Which of the following statements best describes the melodic movement in this first phrase? Tick the box next to your chosen answer.

   ☐ The melody moves entirely by step
   ☐ The melody moves entirely by leap
   ☐ The melody first moves by step and then by leap
   ☐ The melody first moves by leap and then by step

   (b) Name the cadence heard at the end of the first phrase
   ....

   The following questions apply to the entire extract:

   (c) Does the bass part move by step or by leap? ....

   (d) Which instrument plays the bass part? ....

   (e) In what form is this extract? ....

   (f) This extract was written in the classical period. Name one feature heard in the music that suggests this period.
   ....
   ....

Techniques of Melodic Composition   71

3. The first track of Sony, SMK 68331 is the first movement of a 'chamber concerto'. Listen to this track FOUR times before answering the following questions:

(a) Tick one box to indicate which shape best represents the opening melody played by the piano.

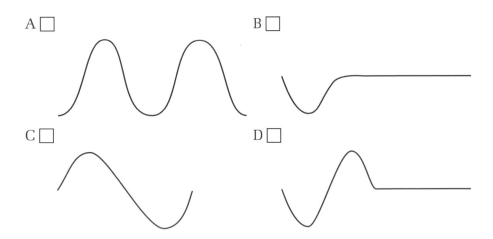

(b) What do you notice about the ensemble that enters following the entries of the piano and then the violin?

   a) It is a symphony orchestra

   b) It is all string instruments

   c) It is all wind instruments

(c) What characteristics of the music tell you it was composed in the 20th century?

....

4. Track 6 on Navras Records Sampler CD No 4 (available from www.navrasrecords.com) is an interpretation of rāg *bhairav*. Listen to this extract THREE times before answering the following questions:

(a) Name **one** instrument you can hear ....

(b) Do you think this extract is from the beginning, middle or end of a rāg performance? ....

Give **two** reasons for your answer.

....

....

(c) Which of the following note patterns do you think the extract is based on? Indicate by ticking one box.

Please note that this example is notated in an approximate pitch. The actual extract sounds slightly flatter than this.

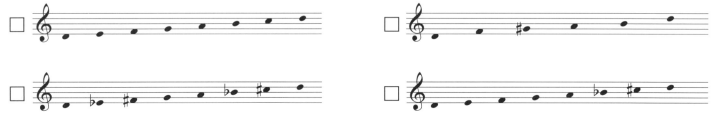

(d) The soloist plays a melodic phrase that is heard throughout the extract in various ways. Describe **one** way in which this phrase is varied.

....

....

72 Techniques of Melodic Composition

Dance Music

Dance is all about movement, which may be relatively spontaneous (as at a rave or a disco) or which may be carefully rehearsed and formal. This second category includes modern line-dance, folk dances, ballroom dances (such as the waltz) and historic dances like the minuet and gavotte. In addition, staged dancing – often in costume and with lighting effects – can be used to tell a story (as in ballet) or to enhance opera, musical shows and spectacular events such as the opening of the Olympic games.

The most important elements in any type of dance music are metre, tempo, rhythm and phrase structure since these all relate directly to the movements of the dancers:

✦ Metre is the way the underlying pulse of music is organised into repeating patterns of strong and weak beats.

✦ Tempo is the speed of the beat. Tempo and metre are both ways in which one type of dance differs from another.

✦ Rhythm refers to the organisation of long and short notes in music. Some dances are characterised by a particular rhythm that features prominently in the music.

✦ Phrase structure: Formal dancing usually involves set movements that are repeated in time to the music. The music itself therefore often consists of regular numbers of symmetrical phrases to which the dance steps can be fitted.

Metre

In dances such as the waltz the beats are in the pattern **strong**–weak–weak. This is called triple metre. The time signature $\frac{3}{4}$ indicates a triple metre of three crotchet beats per bar. Duple metre uses the pattern **strong**–weak. It can be indicated by time signatures such as $\frac{2}{4}$ (two crotchet beats per bar) and $\frac{2}{2}$ or ¢ (two minim beats per bar). Quadruple metre often sounds like two bars of duple metre stuck together, although you may sometimes hear the first of its four beats being given extra emphasis: **strong**–weak–firm–weak. It can be indicated by time signatures such as $\frac{4}{4}$ or **C**.

All of the time signatures mentioned above are known as **simple** because they contain beats that divide into two equal halves when shorter notes are required. If the beats instead divide into three equal portions, the music is said to be in **compound** time. For instance $\frac{6}{8}$ indicates compound duple time – two dotted crotchet beats per bar, each of which can divide into three quavers. In very slow music you might count this as six quaver beats per bar rather than two ♩. beats. An example of compound triple time is $\frac{9}{8}$ (three ♩. beats per bar), while an example of compound quadruple time (four ♩. beats per bar) is $\frac{12}{8}$.

Look at the examples *right* and notice that $\frac{3}{4}$ and $\frac{6}{8}$ can both have six quavers in a bar. The crucial difference is that $\frac{3}{4}$ is simple triple time – three beats per bar, each of which can divide into two – while $\frac{6}{8}$ is compound duple time – two beats per bar, each of which can divide into three. Practise clapping these examples while counting the beats aloud.

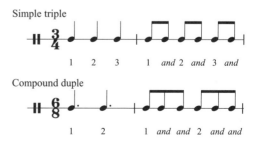

For this Area of Study you need to be familiar with three types of dance music: the Elizabethan pavan and galliard, the Viennese waltz and disco music.

Although music and movement are closely related through the elements described on the previous page, it is important to realise that many dance pieces from past centuries were not intended for actual dancing. Instead they were written to be played in concerts or in the home, where they could evoke the spirit of dance music for the passive listener.

Elizabethan pavan and galliard

The court of Queen Elizabeth I, who reigned from 1558 to 1603, was famous for its music, dance and drama. The queen herself, like her father King Henry VIII, was an accomplished musician.

The pavan and galliard were two of the most important dances of the age. The pavan was slow and in duple metre. The dance movements were stately, and almost processional in character. The pavan was often followed by a galliard. This was a very different type of dance. It was fast and in triple metre. Dotted and syncopated rhythms often contributed to its lively character, as in the example *below*. The dance steps in a galliard involved high jumps, including kicking movements made in mid-air.

Although the two dances are thus highly contrasting they were sometimes based on similar melodic ideas, as in this pavan and galliard by Thomas Morley (1557–c.1602), who was a musician in Queen Elizabeth's Chapel Royal:

The following CDs include examples of pavans and galliards. Those by Susato and Praetorius come from Europe rather than Britain, but are generally similar in style to Elizabethan dances: Holborne *Pavans, galliards and almains* (BIS CD469); Praetorius *Dances from Terpsichore* (L'Oiseau Lyre 414 633-2); Susato *Danserye* (L'Oiseau-Lyre 436 131-2). *Tudor Age Music* (Griffin/Qualiton GCCD 4002) includes a number of pavans and galliards, along with madrigals and other music from the Elizabethan age.

This pavan and galliard can be found in *The Fitzwilliam Virginal Book*, volume two, pages 209–216 (Dover Publications, ISBN 0-486-21069-3).

This pair of dances was written for the virginals, a type of small harpsichord. The double slashes through some note stems indicate ornaments – probably mordents (or brief trills).

The structure of most dances of this period consists of sections that are immediately repeated, usually in a more elaborate variation, producing forms such as AA^{1}BB^{1}CC^1. The variations often consisted of dividing the longer notes in the original melody into scale-like patterns of shorter notes, a technique known as **divisions**. Here are Morley's divisions (A^1) on the first two bars of the pavan illustrated *above*:

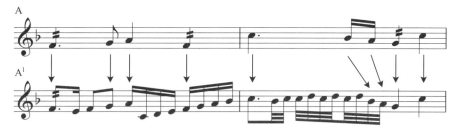

Warning. Photocopying any part of this book without permission is illegal.

74 Dance Music

Another feature of many Elizabethan dances was the formal repetition of the final tonic chord (see *right*). This feature was provided, it is thought, to enable the dancing couples to exchange bows and to conclude their dance in a suitably dignified way. In many recordings of these works you can hear keyboard players improvise elaborate arpeggios on the final chord of these endings.

End of Morley's Galliard

The ornate style of these pieces for virginals suggests that they were intended to be played and listened to at home, rather than danced to publicly. Indeed the virginals would be too quiet to accompany actual dancing, for which a range of other instruments was available.

Elizabethan instruments

In 16th- and 17th-century England an ensemble of solo instruments was known as a consort. There were two types: a whole consort consisted of different sizes of the same instrument (such as the recorder) while a broken consort contained instruments from more than one family.

Consorts often accompanied court dances. Their size could vary. When many people were expected at a dance the consort would contain more (and louder) instruments than would be used for a small-scale dance. Instruments that might have been heard at Elizabeth's court include:

✦ Cornett: a curved wooden instrument with a trumpet-like mouthpiece and finger-holes. There are three different sizes/pitch ranges: cornettino, treble and tenor.

✦ Crumhorn: a hook-shaped wooden instrument with double reed. It has seven finger-holes on the front and one behind. There are four different sizes/pitch ranges: soprano, alto, tenor and bass.

✦ Pipe: a small three-holed instrument usually played along with the tabor (a small drum), by one person.

✦ Recorder: an end-blown flute with finger-holes, originally made from wood. There are several different sizes/pitch ranges of recorder, including descant (or soprano), treble (or alto), tenor and bass.

✦ Lute: a fretted instrument plucked with the fingers. Often compared in shape to a pear cut in half lengthways, the lute's rounded back is made from thin strips of wood. The strings were originally made from gut. They are usually in sets of six pairs (or 'courses'), although the highest-pitched string may be single. The pegbox, which contains the tuning pins, is set almost at right angles to the neck of the instrument. The lute is held across the front of the body with the neck higher than the soundbox.

✦ Theorbo (or chitarrone): a large lute of low pitch. The theorbo was used to enhance the bass lines of dances.

✦ Viol: a bowed instrument with six strings and with seven frets, made from gut, tied across the neck. There are three different members of the viol family: treble, tenor and bass.

Wind

The cornett is not the same as the modern cornet, which is a valved brass instrument and which is spelled with only one 't'.

Strings

> **Warning.** Photocopying any part of this book without permission is illegal.

Dance Music 75

Keyboard

✦ Harpsichord: an instrument in which the strings are plucked with wooden jacks operated from a keyboard. There are several different sizes of harpsichord, some of which have two keyboards and mechanisms called stops with which to alter timbre and pitch. The harpsichord has a shape quite similar to that of a grand piano.

✦ Virginals: a small oblong harpsichord.

20th-century revival

The 20th century saw a revival of the pavan (or pavane) and galliard. The intention of composers here was to create a sense of nostalgia by using old rhythms and structures in a new context. Their compositions were sometimes for symphony orchestra, an ensemble far different from the consorts of Elizabeth's time. On other occasions they were intended for modern instruments such as the piano. The new pavans and galliards also used modern melodic ideas and harmonies. These pieces may give you ideas for your own compositions.

✦ Edward German 'Pavane' from incidental music to *Romeo and Juliet* (available on Marco Polo 8.223419)

✦ Fauré *Pavane*, Op 50 for orchestra with ad lib chorus (Chandos CHAN5416)

✦ Ravel *Pavane pour un Infante Défunte* (EMI 7243 5 68611 2 1)

✦ Ravel 'Pavane de la belle au Bois Dormant' from *Ma Mère l'Oye* (the ballet *Mother Goose*: EMI 7243 5 68611 2 1)

✦ Vaughan Williams 'Pavane of the Heavenly Host' and 'Galliard of the Sons of the Morning' from the ballet *Job* (Classics for Pleasure CD-CCFP4603)

✦ Warlock 'Pavane' from the *Capriol Suite* (Hyperion CDA66938).

Test yourself

1. Briefly explain what is meant by the two following terms:

   Metre ....

   Tempo ....

2. Complete the blanks in these sentences:

   A pavan is in .... metre while a galliard is in .... metre. The tempo of a pavan is .... but the tempo of a galliard is .... The mood of a pavan is .... while the mood of a galliard is ....

3. Only one of these instruments was known in Elizabethan times. Which is it? (Underline your answer.)

   Saxophone   Piano   Recorder   Clarinet

Composing

Write a pavan to accompany the entrance of royalty in a school production of a play by Shakespeare. You can either imitate the style of Elizabethan music or you can write in a modern style, but you must base your piece on the following pavan rhythm:

Warning. Photocopying any part of this book without permission is illegal.

Start with a eight-bar section that you then repeat using the variation technique called divisions (see page 74).

19th-century Viennese waltz

The waltz first became popular in and around Vienna, the capital of Austria, in the 1790s. It went on to become one of the most famous dances in the western world during the 19th century and could be heard not only in ballrooms but also in ballet, opera, orchestral music and in the home (where waltzes were often played on the piano). Even in the 20th century it retained considerable popularity, particularly among composers of light music and musicals. The English waltz (a slow version of the Viennese waltz) is still danced today by those interested in ballroom dancing.

The characteristics of the Viennese waltz include:

✦ Fast triple metre (usually 3/4 time). Waltzes are generally played at about 70 *bars* per minute (♩.=70) and this gives the feel of one beat per bar rather than three. This impression of 'one in a bar' is reinforced through the use of the following:

✦ A slow harmonic pace. This means that the chords change relatively infrequently – the same chord is generally used throughout an entire bar and often remains unchanged for two or even four bars at a time.

✦ Essentially simple harmonies, although often enlivened with melodies that include gently dissonant appoggiaturas and/or colourful chromatic notes.

✦ The use of a **homophonic** texture, in which the emphasis is on a single melodic line with purely supportive accompaniment.

✦ An accompaniment pattern often described as 'um-cha-cha' in which the bass note of a chord occurs on the first beat of the bar and the other notes occur on the second and third beats.

✦ Sections that are built up from phrases of similar length in order to balance one another (as in most types of dance music).

All of these points are illustrated in the following example, which is taken from a set of waltzes for piano written in 1816 by the Austrian composer Schubert, when he was 19 (the original was in A♭ major):

Before the waltz the most popular dance of the 18th century had been the minuet. This was also in 3/4 time, but it was a much more

Warning. Photocopying any part of this book without permission is illegal.

stately dance in which the partners remained literally at arm's length. In the early days of the waltz the movements were often described as 'whirling' – couples rotated in time to the music and male and female partners were pressed closely together as they danced. This last point was of concern to critics of the waltz. Comments were made about the immoral nature of the dance – just as they would be made 150 years later about rock 'n' roll!

The earliest waltzes, such as the one from which the example above is taken, consisted of two repeated eight-bar sections arranged in patterns such as ‖:A:‖:B:‖ (binary form) or ‖:A:‖:BA:‖ (known as rounded binary form).

Usually a number of these short waltzes were grouped together to form a continuous series of dances. Composers would sometimes include pairs of waltzes to be played in the order XYX (ternary form). The central waltz (Y) would generally contrast with the outer parts of this musical sandwich, and was often labelled 'trio' – a term referring to a long-dead practice of scoring a contrasting dance for just a trio of instruments.

> Johann Strauss's three sons – Johann (the younger), Joseph and Eduard – were also famous for their waltzes. The German composer Richard Strauss was not related to this family.

The waltz really took off in popularity after about 1825, particularly due to composers who were also band-leaders, such as Joseph Lanner and Johann Strauss (the elder). Orchestras became larger, waltzes became more sophisticated melodically and harmonically, and structures became longer. A slow introduction, during which the dancing partners got into position, would typically feature the quiet rustling of tremolo strings, harp arpeggios, and evocative fragments of melody on solo wind instruments. This would lead to a series of five or more waltzes in related keys, each now usually constructed from 16- or even 32-bar sections. The set of dances would end with a **coda** which generally referred back to themes heard earlier. These works were quite substantial orchestral pieces and they were often given names to make them more memorable, such as *On the Beautiful Blue Danube*, written by Johann Strauss II in 1867. The *Blue Danube* lasts almost ten minutes and the same composer's *Tales from the Vienna Woods* (1868) is even longer.

> Tempo rubato refers to an expressive 'give and take' in the pulse so that some notes are longer than expected while others are shorter to compensate.

Stylistically, the Viennese waltz was often played with a subtle use of tempo rubato – especially with a slight anticipation of the second beat (the first 'cha'). This anticipation, which was not indicated in the notation, became known as the music's 'breathing space'.

The influence of the waltz

> 'Operetta' is Italian for 'little opera'. It refers to an opera whose words and music are light in mood.

Johann Strauss the younger helped create the Viennese operetta, in which the waltz became an important component. In addition to its role in ballroom scenes, such as the one in Strauss's *Die Fledermaus* (The Bat) composed in 1874, the style of the waltz was also sometimes used in songs. There are a number of these waltz-songs in Franz Lehár's *The Merry Widow* (1905), one of the best-known Viennese operettas, and in the operettas of Gilbert and Sullivan.

Many other 19th-century composers wrote waltzes, although few of such works were intended for the ballroom. Most were written to be played on the piano, which was becoming increasingly popular as an instrument for home entertainment at this time. The 'um-cha-cha' figuration of a waltz accompaniment lends itself well to performance on the piano.

> **Warning.** Photocopying any part of this book without permission is illegal.

Schubert, Schumann, Weber, Chopin and Brahms all composed waltzes of varied length and complexity for the piano. Schumann was intrigued by the image of the masked ball and in the 1830s wrote two sets of piano pieces (*Papillons* and *Carnaval*) based on this idea. In these he sketched in music various real and imaginary characters, capturing their fleeting, anonymous meetings in a series of short movements that include waltzes and other dances.

Other 19th-century composers incorporated waltzes in large-scale orchestral works. In 1830 Berlioz composed a waltz (notated in $\frac{3}{8}$ time) as the second movement of his *Symphonie fantastique*. The first movement of Tchaikovsky's Symphony No. 4 (1878) contains a waltz theme as its principal subject. Here Tchaikovsky helps us realise that the popular dance can be transformed into a melancholy theme within a complex symphonic structure.

Tchaikovsky also included waltzes in his ballets. His *Swan Lake* (1875–6) and *Sleeping Beauty* (1888–9) contain many waltz tunes that remain popular today, and Delibes included waltzes in his ballets *Coppélia* (1870) and *Sylvia* (1876). A number of early 20th-century composers included waltzes in their works (often for ironic effect) and waltzes occur in musicals such as Rogers and Hammerstein's *South Pacific* and Cole Porter's *Kiss Me Kate*.

> A ballet is a dramatic entertainment presented by dancers in costume and often accompanied by an orchestra.

There are hundreds of recordings of 19th-century waltzes. Look out for CDs with titles such as *Favourite Waltzes* that include a good selection of different composers. The precise contents (and CD numbers) of these compilations tend to change quite often, but two well-reviewed selections in recent years were *Favourite Waltzes* (EMI 574767-2) and *Favourite Waltzes* (Decca 417693-2). Look out also for *The Best of Johann Strauss II*, a bargain-price CD from Naxos (8.55664).

Recordings

Test yourself

1. Describe two ways in which you would expect a waltz to sound different from a galliard.

   ....

   ....

2. What is a homophonic texture? ....

   ....

3. Explain what is meant by the following sections in a waltz:

   (a) a trio ....

   (b) a coda ....

4. How would people have heard waltzes in the home in the 19th century?

   ....

Composing

Compose a waltz melody to fit with the following accompaniment. Include at least one chromatic note in your melody. You may find it easier if the accompaniment is first recorded on a sequencer or on tape, so that you can try out your ideas as it plays.

> **Warning.** Photocopying any part of this book without permission is illegal.

Dance Music

If you are a singer you could make your piece a waltz song. If you can't think of any words, here are some by W. S. Gilbert:

Nothing venture, nothing win –
Blood is thick, but water's thin –
In for a penny, in for a pound –
It's love that makes the world go round!

When you are happy with your waltz, add a contrasting 16-bar section in G major. Either invent your own chord scheme for this new section or use the pattern printed *below*. The first section should be played again after this new material, so the piece ends in C major. Finally, write a short introduction to go at the start and a short coda to finish your composition. These two sections could each be four bars long.

Disco music

Disco developed early in the 1970s and laid the foundations of the modern club and dance scene. Disco was created in the USA to meet the needs of young people who attended nightclubs to dance. The improved quality of the equipment used in playing recordings (turntables, amplifiers, loudspeakers) enabled DJs to present music without the need for live musicians. Disco had a mixture of influences from soul to jazz and funk, and soon became the focus of a new dance culture.

Disco clubs brought young people together in a shared experience, yet they were free to dance as individuals, without being constrained by the need for a partner or to follow a dance routine. The clubs provided opportunities for dancers to display contemporary fashions in clothing and accessories.

It was in the disco era that the 12-inch record emerged, meaning that disco songs could be longer than the four or five minutes available previously.

Warning. Photocopying any part of this book without permission is illegal.

The combination of dazzling light effects and amplified sound experienced by dancers was one exciting aspect of disco. Another was the music, which in the 1970s was played on vinyl records and was rhythmically driven. Disco songs typically contained the following musical elements:

- A strongly emphasised pulse, often at about 120 beats per minute
- Clear-cut rhythms which were maintained throughout the song
- A simple verse-and-chorus structure
- A memorable melody and **hook** lines.

The movie *Saturday Night Fever,* starring John Travolta, was released in 1977 with a score by the Bee Gees. The dance scenes on film are lively but, by comparison with later disco and today's dance music, are more formal in terms of their organisation.

The original soundtrack recording of Saturday Night Fever is available on Polydor, 825 389-2.

Form

Structurally a typical disco song consists of some form of instrumental introduction, and then alternating verses and choruses. The verses are usually sung by a soloist and are often **multitracked**. The music for each verse is the same, only the words differ. The choruses are often differentiated from the verses through the use of more voices and/or instruments. Some disco songs start with the chorus (after the introduction) rather than the verse.

Listen to Gloria Gaynor's *Never Can Say Goodbye* (1974). This track provides a fairly typical example of a disco piece – it is in $\frac{4}{4}$ time with an up-beat tempo and has the following structure:

This track is available on Disco Fever (volume 2), Universal 585510-2.

Introduction (instrumental)	Verse		Chorus	Verse		Chorus	Chorus	Instrumental	Chorus
	A	A^1	B	A	A^1	B	B		B
6 bars	8 bars	16 bars	8 bars	8 bars	16 bars	8 bars	8 bars	4 bars	To fade

Strings and trumpets play the instrumental introduction, while during the verses the solo voice is supported primarily by bass and electric guitar and drum kit (trumpets feature towards the end of A^1). The chorus contrasts with the verse as extra voices back up the soloist, the strings perform a decorated melodic line and trumpets support the harmony. Try listening to some other disco tracks and compare their structure and instrumentation with *Never Can Say Goodbye.* For example The Jacksons *Blame it on the Boogie*, Stacy Lattislaw *Jump to the Beat*, Sly and the Family Stone *Dance to the Music*, Village People *YMCA* and Heatwave *Boogie Nights.* Make detailed notes on what you hear.

All of these tracks are available on Disco Fever (volume 1), Universal 556 408-2.

Instrumentation

The solid-bodied electric guitar has six strings, which are sounded with a plectrum. String vibrations are transmitted by electro-magnets, or pickups, to tone-modification circuits and then to an amplifier and loudspeakers. The lead guitar plays mainly solo lines while the rhythm guitar maintains the music's harmonic/rhythmic drive in $\frac{4}{4}$ time.

Lead and rhythm guitar

The electric bass guitar has four strings and the electrical operation of the instrument is similar to that of the lead guitar. The bass guitar maintains a rhythmic bass part derived from the harmonies being used. Short **riffs** are frequently used.

Bass guitar

Warning. Photocopying any part of this book without permission is illegal.

Drum kit and drum machine Drum-kit instruments that feature prominently in disco music are bass drum, snare drum and hi-hat cymbals. The low-pitched bass drum maintains the pulse playing either on every crotchet beat (in $\frac{4}{4}$ time), or on beats 1 and 3. The snare drum typically plays on beats 2 and 4 and sometimes plays more complex rhythmic patterns. Hi-hat cymbals function to emphasise off-beat crotchets or quavers, and sometimes play continuous semiquavers in more upbeat disco songs. Once established, the main drum-kit rhythmic patterns continue largely unchanged during a song.

A drum machine is a specific type of synthesiser designed to produce percussion sounds. It usually incorporates a simple sequencer that enables short rhythm patterns to be stored, edited and replayed automatically.

Dance music and technology

Disco musicians made use of the emerging music technology available, such as mixing and sampling. Some of these techniques and devices are defined below:

MIDI MIDI stands for Musical Instrument Digital Interface, a standard for connecting and remotely operating electronic instruments and related devices such as computers and effects units.

Remix The term remix originally referred to a new version of a recording produced by mixing together the original tracks in different ways, perhaps to give more weight to the bass or to incorporate tracks that were omitted in the original. Nowadays it refers to a new arrangement of a piece, often in a different style.

Sampler A device for recording sections of sound (samples) as digital information. It allows them to be played back with various modifications (eg at different speeds, in continuous loops or in combination with other samples).

Sequencer A sequencer is a device that records, edits and replays electronic performance instructions, such as MIDI-note on and off messages. These instructions are used to control instruments such as synthesisers or samplers.

Looping Much popular dance music, including disco, is based on short fragments of music that are constantly repeated or 'looped'. These loops are typically one, two or four bars long and are usually recorded on a sampler or sequencer. They might consist of a few bass notes, a melodic pattern, some chords or a rhythm. Loops are usually composed so that they can be combined, making it possible to create tension as extra loops are added to the total mix. Some loops may be allocated to specific sections of the piece in order to create contrasting sections such as verses and choruses.

Test yourself

1. In which country did disco develop?

   UK USA Spain France

2. What is the approximate tempo of much disco music in beats per minute (bpm)?

   120 bpm 180 bpm 150 bpm

3. Which two of the following terms accurately describe the basic structure of a disco song?

   Binary   Ternary   Rondo   Verse and chorus

Composing

Write a short song for a disco-dancing competition. The piece must be no longer than two minutes, must be in 4/4 time and must have an upbeat tempo. The lyrics of the song are to be based around the theme of dancing. The song must contain an introduction, two verses and a chorus. You must make use of the bass-guitar riff (shown *right*).

Many disco songs have dancing and having fun as their theme. Try listening to the lyrics of Sly and the Family Stone *Dance to the Music* or Heatwave *Boogie Nights* to get some ideas.

Listening tests

1. Thomas Simpson (1582–1630) published a galliard based on a pavan by Thomas Tomkins (1572–1656). This galliard is track 17 on Naxos, 8.550602 and the Tomkins Pavan in A minor is track 16 on the same CD. Listen to the first 30 seconds of the galliard THREE times before answering the following questions:

(a) What other instrument features as well as viols?

   Organ   Lute   Harpsichord

(b) With which one of the following rhythms does the galliard melody begin?

(c) The extract ends with a slightly delayed, repeated tonic chord. What was the purpose of this repeated chord?

....

2. **A waltz melody by Schubert**

Here is the first section of a waltz melody for piano by Schubert from *Valses sentimentales* D.779 which your teacher will play to you*:

Listen to the melody several times before answering the following questions:

(a) Name the key of the music ....

(b) How would you describe the E♯ in bars 1, 3, 9 and 11?

   The note is diatonic ____

   The note is chromatic ____

   The note is a leading note ____

(c) This section of Schubert's waltz melody is divided into two parts. Write * above the note on which the second part begins.

*In the actual exam all extracts will be played on CD.

3. *When will I see you again?* **by the Three Degrees**

The 1974 hit by the Three Degrees, *When will I see you again?* is on track 17 of CD 2 of *Disco Fever* (Universal 556 408-2). *When will I see you again?* is in 4/4 time and the key of A major. It begins with a 16-bar introduction followed by a verse section (**A**) which is divided into two eight-bar long sections. The chorus (**B**) is unusually short, being four bars in length, but is repeated. Listen to the track THREE times before answering the following questions:

(a) Which of these rhythms correctly represents the rhythm played by the snare drum as the lead into the first bar of the song? Indicate by ticking one box.

(b) The introduction consists of the chords and a similar bass line to that of the first eight bars of the verse section (**A**). Which instruments play the melody during the first eight bars?

Trumpets   Flutes   Violins

(c) Here is an outline of the phrase played by the bass guitar during the first eight-bar section of the verse section. The rhythm is shown but some of the pitches are omitted. Complete the phrase:

(d) Briefly describe how the song ends, following the final verse.

....

....

4. **Donna Summer's *Hot stuff***

Donna Summer's 1979 hit, *Hot stuff*, is on track 5 of CD 1 *Disco fever* (Universal 556 408-2). Listen to the track THREE times before answering the following questions:

(a) Here is an outline of the rhythm of the instrumental melody played before the voice enters at the beginning of verse 1 of *Hot stuff* ('Sittin' here eatin' my heart out, baby'). Some of the notes of the melody are also shown (* indicates a flattened note). Complete the melody by filling in the missing notes:

84   Dance Music

(b) Here are the main rhythms used during the chorus section (B) of *Hot stuff*:

Cymbals
Snare Drum
Bass Drum

Write one sentence on each rhythm describing its musical function:

Cymbal ....

Side drum ....

Bass drum ....

(c) The chords of Cm Dm and Gm are used in the eight-bar chorus (**B**). Write the correct chord in each of the boxes below. The first chord has been given, and the lyrics and bass-drum beat are printed as a guide.

Lyrics Looking for some hot stuff baby this e-vening_____ I need some hot stuff baby tonight_____ I want some

Bass drum

hot stuff baby this e-vening_____ Gotta have some hot stuff Gotta have some love tonight

Traditions and Innovation

In this Area of Study you will focus on salsa, bhangra and minimalism. You will need to be able to identify the key musical features of each style.

Salsa

Salsa is an up-tempo dance style that combines musical traditions from Latin America (mainly from Cuba and Puerto Rico) with American jazz. Salsa literally means 'sauce' – a word shouted out by audiences to reward a particularly hot solo.

The origins of salsa lie in *son*, a type of dance-song from Cuba.

Latin America usually refers to the countries south of the United States, including all of South America. Most of these countries were Spanish colonies at some point, and Spanish became the main language. Spanish-speaking Caribbean countries such as Cuba and Puerto Rico are part of Latin America. Latin music means music from these areas.

The most important thing to understand about *son*, salsa and much other Latin-American music is that it is structured round a rhythmic pattern called clave (pronounced 'clarvay').

Clave patterns

The most common clave pattern comes from the *son* style and is known as *son clave* (see *left*). There are two versions, the 3:2 and the 2:3, depending on whether the group of two or three notes comes first. This pattern is often played on wood sticks called claves (usually pronounced to rhyme with 'caves').

Every musical element is designed to fit in with the clave – it is the central point that all the other parts relate to. All performers in a salsa/*son* band would be aware of the relevant type of clave pattern for each piece and know how their part fitted with it. The clave rhythm can be felt throughout much Latin music, even when it is not actually played.

Claves

Look at the music for *The Peanut Vendor* by Simmons, Sunshine and Gilbert:

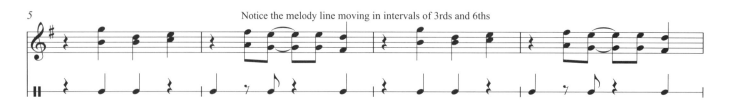

There is a simple arrangement of *The Peanut Vendor* available on Muzika EM101.

This is a classic *son* tune and the melody clearly fits with the clave rhythm – be aware though that not all *son* and salsa tunes fit quite so clearly with the clave as here. Try recording the melody (or play it into a keyboard/computer), and then clap the clave pattern in both 3:2 and 2:3 versions. You should find that the 2:3 version printed *above* fits much better than the 3:2 version.

Que Pista is track 10 from *The Rough Guide to Cuban Son* (World Music Network, RGNET1046).

Try this exercise again with *Que Pista* printed on page 87. This track features the Cuban band Los Van Van (who mix traditional *son* styles with electric bass and synthesisers – they call their

86 Traditions and Innovation

music *songo*). The clave rhythm is not played, but the melody fits very closely with the *son clave*. Try playing the clave part below in time with the recording:

Different dance styles may have different clave patterns. In rumba the last note of the three-note bar of the clave is a quaver later (see right), giving the music quite a different rhythmic feel. An example is *Anda Ven Y Muévete*.

Anda Ven Y Muévete is available on *Los Van Van (La Colleción Cubana)*, which is issued on the Nascente label (NSCD040).

Cuban son

Son is an old Cuban dance-song style recently given a new lease of life through the international success of Buena Vista Social Club, a recording of traditional tunes by old-time Cuban musicians (several in their seventies or even eighties). The forms and rhythms of *son* are the most important influence on modern salsa music. Once you have listened to a few examples you should begin to recognise the key features of *son* quite quickly:

✦ The music is based around the *son clave* pattern

✦ Other Latin-American percussion instruments (such as maracas and bongos) interact with the clave, forming complex **cross-rhythms**

✦ There is much use of call and response between lead singer (*pregón*) and chorus (*chóro*)

✦ Melodies often move in intervals of 3rds and 6ths (see *The Peanut Vendor*)

✦ Harmonies are usually simple, based around primary chords (chords I, IV and V – in C major these would be C, F and G)

✦ Frequent use of ostinato patterns, often based on syncopated rhythms

✦ In the bass part the last note of a bar often anticipates the harmony of the next bar, giving a syncopated feel.

Son contains features from the traditional music of both Africa and Spain.

African elements include:

✦ Complex cross-rhythms

✦ Call and response between solo singer and chorus

✦ Use of percussion instruments of African origin, including bongo drums, claves and maracas.

Listen out for the clave pattern in any of these recordings, and then try clapping it in time with the music:

Rough Guide to Salsa (World Music Network, RGNET1017), tracks 8 and 12

Rough Guide to Salsa Dance (World Music Network, RGNET1035), tracks 8 and 14

Rough Guide to Cuban Son (World Music Network, RGNET1046), tracks 3, 11 and 14

Mi Terra, Gloria Estefan, (Epic, EPC 4737992), track 5

Buena Vista Social Club, (World Circuit, WCD050), track 3

Tin Tin Deo, Dizzy Gillespie (Verve, 5490862), track 12.

Musicians talk of 'Afro-Cuban music' to describe this fusion of different styles. The slave trade forcibly took many Africans to the Caribbean so it is not surprising to find African musical influences at work in Cuba. The Spanish element in Cuban music is very strong and stems from the days when Cuba was a Spanish colony.

Warning. Photocopying any part of this book without permission is illegal.

Traditions and Innovation 87

Spanish elements include:

✦ The tonal style of the music, with melodies harmonised in 3rds and 6ths

✦ Language and style of the lyrics

✦ Use of the *tres* (a Cuban instrument with three pairs of strings, modelled on the Spanish guitar).

The structure of *son* is another important influence on salsa. An opening verse (or set of verses) is followed by a *montuno* section, where the lead singer or instrumentalist improvises, answered by the *chóro*. In the *montuno* section the bongo player traditionally changes to the cowbell.

Traditional son bands

Early bands included the *sexteto*, which consisted of six instruments (guitar, *tres*, bass, bongos, maracas and claves) plus a singer. Later these bands developed into larger ensembles.

The influence of jazz

> Try to listen to recordings of the bands led by Count Basie.

While *son* is the main root of salsa the other major influence comes from American big-band jazz.

> The frontline section is often referred to as the horn section, and can comprise any mix of melodic instruments. Don't be confused by references to horns in your further reading.

The standard big-band line-up consists of frontline instruments that have a melodic role, usually divided into sections of trumpets, trombones and reeds (saxophones and clarinet) and a rhythm section with piano, double bass, guitar and drum kit.

For GCSE you may need to know about the main instruments and features of the big band (especially popular in the 1930s and 1940s) although be aware that only some of these features are regularly found in salsa.

Some features of big-band music include:

✦ Syncopated rhythms

✦ Frequent use of complex chords (for example 7ths, 9ths, and chords with added or altered notes)

✦ **Riffs**

✦ Dialogue between different sections of the band

✦ Walking bass (a bass part in steady crotchets that outlines the harmony by using notes from the current chord, often filled in with passing notes)

✦ **Comping** – the rhythmic playing of chords on piano/guitar to accompany a soloist or a tune played by the whole band

✦ Brilliant arrangements for instruments in close harmony.

Dizzy Gillespie was one of several musicians who became interested in the fusion of Afro-Cuban music with jazz. It was the updating of this Latin-jazz style by New York-based Latin-American musicians that led directly to salsa.

> All extracts mentioned here are from *Ken Burns' Jazz: Dizzy Gillespie*, Verve 549 086-2.

Listen to Dizzy Gillespie's *Birks' Works*. The standard big-band line-up (except for guitar) is featured on this track. After a short introduction the main tune (head) is heard (0'14"). The music uses complex jazz harmonies and is syncopated. Try counting 1–2–3–4

88 Traditions and Innovation

at the start and feel how many notes are on the off beat. The first solo comes in at 1'14" and underneath the saxophone you can clearly hear a walking bass, the piano comping and the classic ride-cymbal swing rhythm. The head comes back at 4'18". Notice the screamingly high trumpet playing which is characteristic of Dizzy Gillespie.

Dizzy Gillespie's *Manteca* (track 10) shows his interest in Afro-Cuban music through the use of congas alongside the more conventional big-band line-up. Also reminiscent of Afro-Cuban music is the way the sections of the band answer each other, which can be clearly heard from 0'38". *Tin Tin Deo* (track 12) is another Latin-influenced piece (including congas) but for a smaller ensemble. A 3:2 *son clave* pattern can clearly be heard.

Congas are tall, narrow drums from Cuba that are played with the fingers.

Salsa bands usually have:

- A small frontline (brass and/or saxophones)
- Vocals (lead singer and chorus)
- A rhythm section consisting of piano, guitar, bass
- Latin percussion (timbales, drum kit, congas, bongos, maracas, güiro).

Salsa bands

A few salsa bands and artists to listen out for are Celia Cruz, Eddie and Charlie Palmieri, Fruko y sus Tesos, Oscar D'Leon and Cubanismo.

Each section of the band has its own role and this leads to a web of complex cross-rhythms, based around clave patterns. You are also likely to hear dialogue (the passing of phrases from one section of the band to another), and call and response between the vocal soloist and other singers. The music is nearly always structured around ostinato patterns/riffs. Jazz-influenced instrumental solos as well as the more traditional vocal improvisation are both likely to be found in the *montuno* section.

There are lots of MIDI files of salsa tunes on the internet. Try using www.google.com to search for a piece called *Toca Bonito*.

Don't worry if you don't hear all of these features in every piece. Salsa is a broad term covering a range of styles. In some salsa pieces you can hear the *son* influence clearly. Other pieces are based on a wide range of dance styles from all over Latin America. Some salsa pieces are more heavily jazz-influenced than others.

Test yourself on salsa

1. What is the rhythmic pattern found in salsa called?
   ....

2. What is *son*?
   ....

3. Name four Latin-American percussion instruments.
   ....
   ....

4. What performance technique might a soloist use in the *montuno* section of *son* and salsa?
   ....

5. Which famous jazz musician explored the fusion of Afro-Cuban music with jazz?
   ....

Warning. Photocopying any part of this book without permission is illegal.

One of your compositions for GCSE Music has to be based on techniques from one of the core styles in Areas of Study 3 or 4.

There are lots of examples of composers/artists using salsa/Latin-American music blended with other styles.

Salsa/Latin music blended with	Artist/ Composer	Key Piece
Rock	Santana	Oye Como Va
Pop	Gloria Estefan	Mi Tierra
Classical	Gershwin	Cuban Overture
Broadway Musical	Bernstein	West Side Story ('America')
	Frank Loesser	Guys and Dolls ('Havana')
Jazz	Dizzy Gillespie	Manteca/ Tin Tin Deo
	Cubanismo	Mardi Gras Mambo

Warning. Photocopying any part of this book without permission is illegal.

Composing

If Latin music appeals to you, then you may want to try writing a salsa piece of your own. Alternatively you might try combining some of the Latin-American techniques with your other musical interests. You must make it clear that you are using musical techniques that you have learned from your study of salsa.

✦ Write a salsa piece with verses followed by a *montuno* section in an improvisatory style.

✦ Compose a tune in 3rds and 6ths that fits with a *son clave* pattern (like *The Peanut Vendor* – see page 86).

✦ Compose a piece using Latin percussion rhythms (as in *No Gracias* on page 93) with call-and-response patterns for two voices (or groups of voices) on top.

✦ Use the *son montuno* rhythm in the piano and bass part for *No Gracias* in a classical, jazz or popular style.

✦ Design a piece based on different ostinato patterns that form complex cross-rhythms when performed together. Use a clave pattern as the fixed point which locks with all the other rhythms.

✦ Write a song that uses clave rhythms in the accompaniment (for example a piano or rhythm-guitar part) and a bass line that anticipates the chord in the following bar.

Any of these suggestions could work for live instruments, voices, music technology or a mixture. Use these as starting points to create your own music, but make it clear (in your composing brief) exactly which salsa techniques you have used.

No Gracias: a template for composing and performing your own salsa piece

No Gracias (see page 93) illustrates many of the characteristic features and patterns of salsa. It is based on traditional *son montuno* dance rhythms. Try to play this with your GCSE group or produce a sequenced version using a computer or keyboard. You can perform the piece with almost any wind, string or brass instrument playing the 'horn' parts, with or without voices. If you have not played any Latin music before, you may find it difficult to fit the different syncopated patterns together at first. The key to this is quite literally the clave pattern. This has been written out above the score for *No Gracias*.

Before you try to get this piece working as a group, practise your own part. Record the clave pattern on a tape recorder, keyboard or computer **sequencer**. Play or sing your part against it until you are sure that your performance will 'lock' with the clave beat. The hardest parts are probably the piano and bass. These use traditional *son* dance rhythms. If you look at the piano part you will see that in each two-bar pattern only the first two notes come on the beat – everything else is off-beat. It can be really hard to play this in time especially if you are trying to play it against a count of 1–2–3–4. This is where the clave comes in. Look at the piano part and work out exactly which notes come at the same time as a clave

90 Traditions and Innovation

beat – if you listen carefully to the clave and make sure that these notes lock with it, then you will be able to keep in time.

Performing exercises

Whatever instrument you play it is good practise to try playing, singing or clapping all of the parts for *No Gracias* against the clave.

1. Record the clave beat. Practice playing the right-hand line of the piano part (on any instrument, or voice) against the clave beat (see example *below*). Do this slowly at first so that you can consciously think about matching the right notes to the clave.

2. Replay the clave pattern at different speeds until you can play the piano part in time with the clave at a reasonable speed. You will probably find this difficult, but stick with it – if you can feel this rhythm it will really help you to play Latin music.

3. If you want a real challenge, try playing the piano part while tapping your foot to the clave pattern. This may seem impossible at first but if you keep working at it one day it will suddenly seem easy (honestly!) and then you really will have the key to Latin music.

4. Try this exercise with each of the parts to *No Gracias*. With the bass part, it may be necessary to try playing at first without the ties, when the even-numbered bars will fit in with the 'three' side of the clave pattern (see example).

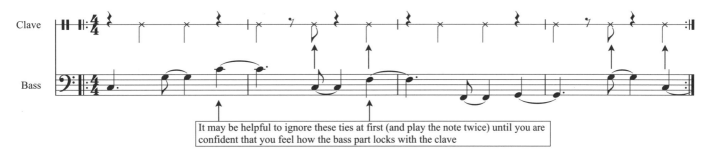

It may be helpful to ignore these ties at first (and play the note twice) until you are confident that you feel how the bass part locks with the clave

5. The other parts should seem easy if you managed to get the piano rhythm right.

How to rehearse *No Gracias*

1. Firstly try the exercises listed above. Then practise your part individually, and make sure you can play absolutely in time with the clave.

2. Practise the Latin percussion parts shown on page 92. The example shows classic son/salsa percussion patterns that you can use with *No Gracias*. Practise the percussion parts until they 'lock' solidly with the clave. You really can't go any further until you have got this in place. If you don't have many percussion instruments or if you find this difficult it may be

Warning. Photocopying any part of this book without permission is illegal.

worth using a computer sequencer to provide a percussion backing to perform with. You can get Latin percussion sounds using the drum settings on most keyboards and computer soundcards.

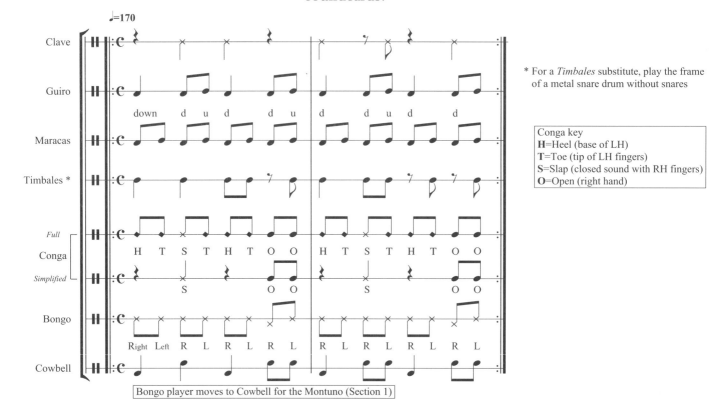

3. Create an introduction before verse 1 in which the instruments enter gradually in the following order:

    ✦ Clave

    ✦ Other percussion

    ✦ Bass

    ✦ Piano/guitar

    ✦ Horns and vocals.

4. Practise the verse next.

5. Move on to the *montuno* section. The piano, bass and percussion parts stay exactly the same in this section. Practise taking it in turns to improvise in the four bars at the start of the montuno. Because the chóro and horns will answer your improvisation, you will need to make sure it matches the style of their music. If you have not done much improvising before, listen to as much salsa as you can to try to pick up the style.

6. Perform the piece. Try this structure: Intro (rhythm section) – Verse (twice) – Montuno – Verse. Above all have fun with it – if it doesn't have a real rhythmic kick and it isn't fun then it isn't salsa.

7. Now try composing your own salsa piece using some of the rhythms and patterns seen in *No Gracias*.

Warning. Photocopying any part of this book without permission is illegal.

92 Traditions and Innovation

Salsa features in *No Gracias*

No Gracias demonstrates many of the key features of salsa:

✦ The piano, bass, percussion and horn/vocal parts each have their own rhythms – the 2:3 clave pattern is the key that locks all of these cross rhythms together

✦ The whole piece is based on syncopated ostinato patterns – the piano and bass part do exactly the same thing throughout

✦ The piano and bass use a classic *son* rhythm, with most notes off beat

✦ There is an opening set of verses (*No Gracias* only has one) followed by a *montuno* section with call and response between the solo improvisers and the horns/chorus

✦ The melody for voices and 'horns' is often split into two parts which sound a 3rd or a 6th apart

✦ There is call and response between the lead singer and chóro

✦ The bass part characteristically has the last note of a bar anticipating the chord heard in the next bar.

A full version of *No Gracias* with full text and translation can be downloaded from the Rhinegold Study Guides website: www.rhinegold.co.uk.

Warning. Photocopying any part of this book without permission is illegal.

Traditions and Innovation 93

Bhangra

Bhangra originated as a folk dance from the Punjab region of north India and Pakistan, where it was performed to celebrate the end of the harvest. The music is led by the *dhol*, a double-sided wooden barrel drum – one side has much more of a bass sound than the other. The *dhol* provides a driving beat. This is music for celebration and the dance steps of bhangra reflect its harvest origins.

The rhythm that dominates both traditional and modern bhangra is known as *chaal*:

The *dhol* can be heard as a solo instrument (with characteristic shouts of 'Hoi') on track 7 of *Bhangra Beatz* (Naxos World 76012-2).

The words are part of a system in Indian music called *bols* (words to help you remember drum patterns). Both sides of the *dhol* are played on the notes marked 'dha', while only the treble side is struck on the notes marked 'na'. The word 'ge' is used if only the bass side of the drum is to be struck.

Chaal is an eight-note pattern. The importance of rhythmic cycles (known as *tal*) in Indian music has already been mentioned (see page 69). Notice that the *bols* only indicate drum strokes, and not the rhythm. As you can see from the western notation above, the rhythm itself has a shuffle feel, rather like swung quavers in jazz.

The GCSE specification also refers to a rhythm actually called 'bhangra'. Despite the name it seems much less obvious in bhangra music than the chaal rhythm:

Practise playing this rhythm until you are sure that you will recognise it whenever you hear it. If you can get hold of a double-headed drum use that – if not any drum (or even a desk) will do. Use both hands together for the *dha* strokes and one hand only for *na*. You should be able to feel how the two-handed strokes give a real kick to the rhythm.

Modern bhangra developed in the Asian communities of the UK and fuses traditional dance rhythms and tunes of the east with club-dance culture. As people from Asia moved to settle in Britain they brought their own musical cultures and over time these merged with western popular music. Bhangra was first heard in the UK when amateur bands played for Asian weddings (or other celebrations) – it later developed into a more commercial form. Modern bhangra uses traditional rhythms and tunes with western instruments such as bass, electric guitar and keyboards.

The Rough Guide to Bhangra is on the World Music Network label (RGNET 1054CD).

Alaap was one of the first bhangra bands to become popular in the UK. In the early 1980s their song *Bhabiye Ni Bhabiye* was the first bhangra hit single in the UK and it is regularly played at Asian weddings even today. This song is an example of a relatively traditional bhangra sound and is about a man asking his sister-in-law to find him a beautiful girl like herself that he can marry. If you listen to this track (on *The Rough Guide to Bhangra*) you can clearly hear *chaal* rhythms played on the *dhol*. You can also hear shouts of 'Hoi' – another characteristic feature of bhangra.

Warning. Photocopying any part of this book without permission is illegal.

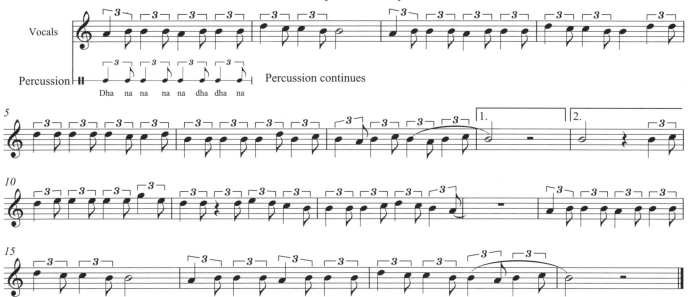

More recently bhangra has combined traditional elements with western popular-music styles such as rap, reggae, hip-hop, disco and drum 'n' bass. Bhangra tracks can sound very different from each other because of the different popular-music influences involved. Music technology plays an important part in modern bhangra, including the use of sampling, remix, effects and sequencing. A drum machine often replaces the *dhol*, but the basic bhangra beat survives. In all of its forms bhangra is dance music – a real fusion of dance cultures across both place and time.

As in much recent popular music, bhangra musicians make use of samples. These are recordings of short extracts from other recordings (such as part of a bass line or drum part) or sometimes words and sounds (such as the dialogue from a film). These samples are then combined with new music.

Sampling

Malkit Singh's *Boliyan* uses a wide range of samples – film extracts, classical music and dance music patterns. Labh Janjua and Panjabi MC's *Mundian To Bach Ke* uses a sampled version of the Busta Rhymes/Knightrider theme (originally from a 1980s television show). You can also hear the DJ technique known as 'scratching' at the end of this track.

Boliyan is track 5 on *The Rough Guide to Bhangra*.

This music is included in the *Rough Guide to Bhangra*, track 13.

In pop music the different layers (such as drums, bass, guitars and vocals) are often recorded one track at a time. This is known as multitrack recording. In a remixed version (see page 82) these tracks are combined and balanced in different ways, with some parts being left out and new tracks added. This often changes the style of the music considerably.

Remix

Piya Re Piya Re is a remixed version of music by Nusrat Fateh Ali Khan. The original is in a style known as qawwali, but the remix has added bhangra beats that give the music a quite different feel. A traditional bhangra version of *Hey Jamalo* followed by a remixed version by Bally Sagoo can be heard on the CD accompanying *Music Worldwide*.

Qawwali is a style of Islamic devotional music popularised in the west by the singer Nusrat Fateh Ali Khan. *Piya Re Piya Re* is track 9 on *The Rough Guide to Bhangra*.

Music Worldwide by Elizabeth Sharma is published by Cambridge University Press, ISBN 0-521-37622-X.

Traditional bhangra is an example of north-Indian popular culture. There are plenty of other examples of fusions between British and

Other British-Asian fusions

Traditions and Innovation **95**

Asian music and many of these relate to the Indian classical music tradition. We will look at how these elements have been combined with western styles.

George Harrison of the Beatles became interested in Indian music and had lessons with the sitar player Ravi Shankar. His 1967 song *Within You, Without You* (on the *Sgt Pepper's Lonely Hearts Club Band* album) features the following elements of Indian music:

- Instruments such as sitar, tabla (see page 69) and tanpura
- A drone (played on the tanpura)
- Melodies based around rāgs
- Tabla patterns based around tāls.

> The composer Gustav Holst was interested in Indian (especially Hindu) culture and many of his pieces reflect this, such as *Savitri* and the *Choral Hymns from the Rig Veda*.

The British jazz guitarist John McLaughlin became interested in Indian music and his band Shakti shows a genuine and sympathetic fusion between Indian music and jazz.

Talvin Singh is a classically trained tabla player, producer and remix artist. His music blends traditional Indian influences (from the classical tradition to bhangra) with a range of western dance styles (such as drum 'n' bass, techno and ambient).

> The bhangra influence (and *chaal* rhythm) is very clear on the *Mustard Fields* track from Talvin Singh's *Ha* (Omni, B00005AA36) album. *OK* is available on Omni, B0000DI1W.

Listen to *Eclipse* (track 6) on Talvin Singh's *OK* album. The mix of styles is immediately apparent, with classical Indian drones and tabla playing mixed with samples, electronic sounds and effects (FX). You can also hear the style of singing associated with qawwali.

Test yourself on bhangra

1. In which region of India and Pakistan did traditional bhangra originate?

   ....

2. What percussion instrument is associated with bhangra?

   ....

Performing

With other members of your GCSE group make up your own cover version of *Bhabiye Ni Bhabiye*. Use the printed music on page 95 as a starting point and play or sing the main tune over the *chaal* rhythm. Then try improvising tunes of your own in a similar style over the drum rhythms.

Try using the bhangra mixer at www.punjabonline.com/java/mixer1/jmusic.html to provide a backing for your performance. This website provides samples of typical bhangra patterns.

Use an electronic keyboard or computer program (such as the *Dance eJay* series) to create drum tracks in various western dance styles such as reggae or disco. Perform the melody of *Bhabiye Ni Bhabiye* with each until you find a rhythmic style that seems to suit the song. See if you can get the *chaal* rhythm to fit as well.

Composing

The fact that modern bhangra draws together so many different styles means that there are lots of potential starting points for your own composing work. You will need to show that you are using a range of techniques drawn from the bhangra music that you have studied and make this clear in your composing brief.

Here are some suggestions:

- Compose a melody in the style of *Bhabiye Ni Bhabiye* and combine it with a dance-music backing.

- Compose a piece for instruments (or voice) and drums based around the *chaal* rhythm.

- Compose a piece that combines western instruments with sounds from Indian music created with music technology. You could use software (such as *Swar Shala*) that offers samples of Indian music or appropriate sounds on an electronic keyboard, or a sequencer like Logic or Cubase to access sitar sounds on a computer or synthesiser.

- Create a piece using the *chaal* rhythm that also involves effects such as reverb or distortion. If you don't have access to music technology to do this use your imagination to come up with ways of altering the sound of an instrument or voice. Try playing a trumpet into different types of dustbin; singing into a piano with the sustaining pedal held down; playing a grand piano with lots of ping-pong balls sitting on the strings.

- Create a piece that uses classical Indian melodic or rhythmic patterns (rāg and tāl) over a drone. You can find several tāl patterns (available as freely downloadable MIDI files) on www.ancient-future.com/theka.html or www.santoor.com/instruction1.html.

Quick Guide to Dance Music by Ian Waugh (PC Publishing 2000) shows you how to build up backings for styles such as disco, hip-hop, garage, drum 'n' bass, and techno.

Swar Shala is a piece of software that contains samples of indian instruments and rhythmic/melodic patterns. It is available from www.swarsystems.com/SwarShala/, although it is rather expensive.

Although large, the piano is a sensitive instrument, and can be damaged by something as simple as greasy fingers touching the strings. Always ask before attempting this sort of project.

Minimalism

Minimalism is a style of art music that developed in the 1960s and 1970s. In some ways minimalist music is very simple, relying on what appear to be endless repetitions (or loops) of simple material. Although it may initially appear simple such music often turns out to be highly complex, certainly in terms of rhythm.

The harmonies in minimal music tend to stay the same for long periods of time and there is little that could be called a melody. The interest comes from subtle changes to the rhythm and texture of the repeated patterns. In this style the ear focuses on very small alterations to a repeated pattern (for example one note changing at a time).

You may think this sounds boring, but at its best minimalist music has a hypnotic quality. In many cases the main musical material could literally be written on the back of a postcard – it is the constant slight changes to the patterns over time that hold the listener's interest.

Try listening to Steve Reich's *Clapping Music* (on *Early Works*, Nonesuch, 7559791692) and John Adams' *Shaker Loops* (on *Minimalist*, The Classics VM5618512).

Minimalist techniques

Here are some of the techniques you will find in minimalist music. Try to use them in your own compositions:

- Additive melody. Adding (or subtracting) a note to/from a

Warning. Photocopying any part of this book without permission is illegal.

pattern on repetition. A similar technique is to replace notes gradually in a repeated pattern with rests, or rests with notes.

Philip Glass: *Music in 5ths*
Additive melody – one extra quaver is added to the pattern each time.

- Phase shifting. Two or more performers start by playing the same pattern. A note or rest is then added to (or removed from) one part to change the length of its pattern slightly. This part will then gradually move out of, and eventually back in, phase with the other part.

Phase shifting: the repeating pattern in the top part is four beats long. In the lower part a crotchet rest has been added, creating a five-beat pattern which moves in and out of phase with the top part.

Lower part shifts out of phase   *Lower part back in phase*

- Layering of ostinato patterns of different lengths (eg three- and four-beat patterns, played at the same time). This is a variation on phase shifting, leading to the patterns coming in and out of phase with each other.

- Metamorphosis. Ostinato patterns that gradually change. The changes are often minimal – a single note or rhythm at a time. The texture of the music might also change by gradually getting more or less complicated.

John Adams: *Tromba Lontana* (adapted)
Ostinato patterns gradually changing over time

Notice how the patterns gradually move away from the original harmonies and then return. In most bars only one note is changed.

Music technology and minimalism

Minimalism and music technology have always gone hand in hand. In the 1960s Terry Riley and Steve Reich were experimenting with tape loops. Music or speech was recorded on to magnetic tape and a portion of the tape was then cut off and stuck together in a loop. To play the loop, the tape was run out of the tape recorder around a bottle or microphone stand and back into the recorder. This was an important technique at the time – things are rather easier nowadays: software on your computer will loop the music for you.

In Steve Reich's *Electric Counterpoint* (1987) a guitarist uses multitracking to record up to ten guitar parts and two electric bass parts. When multitracking in this way the performer will record one track at a time while listening to what has already been recorded through headphones. In concert the final guitar part is then played live against the tape backing.

Electric Counterpoint and *Different Trains* are available on *Elektra/Nonesuch* (7559-79176-2).

In *Different Trains* (1988) Steve Reich recorded train sounds and people talking about their experience of travel by rail. Short snippets from these sounds were then recorded on to tape and repeated several times. This is a process a bit like sampling. In performance a live string quartet plays alongside the tape recorder. The string parts imitate the patterns of the speech 'samples'. What makes this piece really powerful and moving is that in the second movement the recorded voices come from survivors of the second world war concentration camps, talking of their experiences.

Many minimalist composers were influenced by non-western music, particularly west-African drum music, gamelan (percussion orchestras from Bali and Java) and Indian classical music.

Non-western influences

The Amadinda xylophone tradition from Uganda combines simple ostinato patterns to produce complex rhythms. See www.tidewater.net/~xylojim/edwood.html for details.

Steve Reich studied in west Africa and his piece *Drumming* is directly related to drumming techniques from Ghana. He was also influenced by Balinese gamelan. Terry Riley and Philip Glass studied Indian classical music. This experience had a direct impact on their own compositions – you may find that the music you study for GCSE has the same effect on you.

Drumming is available on Nonesuch, 7559791702.

The following table shows some ways in which non-western music may have influenced minimalist composers. Bear in mind that influences on composers are many and varied, and that these suggestions are bound to be a simplification of the actual process.

Features of minimalism	Possible influence from non-western music
Constant repetition (looping or ostinato)	Much non-western music is based around repeating cycles. This is true of gamelan, west-African drumming and Indian classical music (for example, the concept of tāl).
The music often has a hypnotic quality – pieces can last for a long time	Performances of non-western music often last for hours (for example gamelan and Indian classical music).
The interest of the music does not relate to the harmony; harmonies often stay the same for a long time	In Indian classical music a drone continues right through a performance. The interest of gamelan music does not relate to the harmony.
Polyrhythms	In west-African drum music the individual parts form complex rhythms when played together.
Layering of different rhythms on top of each other	In gamelan, there are several layers of sound moving at different rates. The smaller, higher-pitched instruments play many more notes than the large gongs.
Interest is often largely rhythmic, focusing on patterns changing over time	West-African drum music features complex percussion rhythms built around a bell pattern. A master drummer signals changes in the rhythmic patterns.

Gamelan music is based on a texture called **heterophony**, in which different versions of the same core melody are played simultaneously. This is reflected in minimalism where the changing texture is often more important than melody or harmony. The following example shows a minimalist style based on the heterophonic texture of gamelan (the gong parts aren't shown):

Warning. Photocopying any part of this book without permission is illegal.

Higher pitched instruments

Core melody

Notice how all parts relate to the core melody, but each moves at a different rate. The higher pitches play faster notes.

Gamelan music is not normally shown in western notation.

Test yourself

1. Define the following minimalist techniques:

   a) additive melody

   ....
   ....

   b) phase shifting

   ....
   ....

2. In which century did minimalist music develop?

   ....

3. Name two ways that gamelan music may have influenced minimalist composers.

   ....
   ....

Composing

When using minimalist techniques remember to make it clear in your composing brief which features of minimalism you will be using. Music technology can be a great help in minimalist music, especially if you are using complex phase-shifting rhythms. Make sure that you don't rely too much on exact repetition. The loop button on a computer sequencer can be a bit too easy to use sometimes. Good minimalist pieces use subtle transformation of ideas rather than exact repetition.

Here are some suggestions for starting points:

1. Compose a piece using any of the minimalist techniques described on pages 97–98. You could compose for voices, instruments, music technology or any combination of these.

2. Write a piece that combines live sound with pre-recorded music (as in *Electric Counterpoint*). You could use a computer sequencer or multitrack recorder to build up a backing and then compose parts for members of your GCSE group to play or sing on top.

3. Record people talking. Pick out some characteristic phrases and try to translate the pitch and rhythm of them into music.

Warning. Photocopying any part of this book without permission is illegal.

4. Compose a piece using techniques found in gamelan or west-African drumming.

5. Listen to the type of ostinato patterns that Philip Glass uses in much of his music (such as the second movement of his violin concerto) and then compose a piece where a long tune is played over similar slowly changing patterns.

Glass's Concerto for Violin and Orchestra is available on Naxos, 8554568.

Fusion in classical music

You have been exploring music that draws together influences from different cultures by focusing on three music styles all dating from the last half-century. But of course there are plenty of examples of earlier composers using traditional folk music in their pieces. Composers such as Vaughan Williams, Smetana, Tchaikovsky and Bartók either used traditional folk tunes or made use of particular features of the folk-music style of their own country. Dvořák and Smetana regularly used Czech dance rhythms: listen to Dvořák's *Slavonic Dances* for examples. Vaughan Williams not only used traditional tunes but was influenced by the modal style of much English folk music. His *Five Variants of 'Dives and Lazarus'* are variations on a modal folk tune. In most cases the composers were building on folk traditions to try to create an orchestral musical style distinctive to their own country.

Dvořák's Slavonic Dances is available on Teldec (8573810382).

See pages 56–59 for more on modal music.

Five Variants of 'Dives and Lazarus' is available on Naxos (8550323).

Other classical composers made deliberate use of features from different cultures. Both Mozart and Haydn were influenced by what they knew of Turkish music. Haydn's Symphony No. 100 introduced audiences to the sound of bass drum and cymbals – instruments that came from Turkish music. Mozart's Piano Sonata in A K331, third movement, is marked Rondo alla Turca. Notice the rapid left-hand arpeggios: do you hear how they suggest the cymbals and bass drum? In the 20th century Debussy, Ravel and Britten were all influenced by the Indonesian gamelan, and made use of gamelan techniques in their own music. 'Pagodes' from Debussy's *Estampes* is a good example of gamelan influence on a western composer.

Haydn's Symphony No. 100 is available on Telarc, CD 80282; Mozart's Piano Sonata in A K331 is available on Philips, 4121232; and Debussy's Estampes on Naxos, 8.223751.

Listening tests

Salsa

1. Listen to Orquesta Aragón's *El Baile del Suavito* (track 9) THREE times before answering the following questions:

Both salsa extracts are from The Rough Guide to Cuban Son (World Music Network RGNET 1046).

(a) Identify the ostinato pattern played by the piano at the start of this track. Tick your answer.

(b) Which of the following best describes the piano part throughout the whole track?

☐ The piano plays exactly the same rhythm and pitches all the way through

☐ The piano plays exactly the same rhythm all the way through but on different pitches

☐ The piano plays the same rhythm and pitches for most of the time with some breaks and a solo

☐ The piano part is constantly changing throughout the piece

(c) Name three instruments that you can hear apart from the percussion and piano.

....

2. Listen to *No Me Digas Corazon* (track 11) THREE times before answer the following questions:

(a) Name instrument (a) that plays the printed music above, heard at the start of this track.

....

(b) Name the instrument (b) that enters in bar 4. ....

(c) After the example printed above has been played twice, claves join in with this same music. Write down this clave rhythm on the line provided above.

(d) This extract is an example of Cuban *son*. Describe three features that you hear that are characteristic of this musical style.

....
....
....
....
....
....

Bhangra

3. Listen to one minute of *Chargiye* by Bombay Talkie THREE times before answering the following questions:

Chargiye is track 3 on *The Rough Guide to Bhangra* (RGNET 1054).

(a) Describe two musical features of bhangra that you hear.

....
....

(b) Describe two features of western popular music that you hear.

....
....

(c) The main vocal tune is heard from 0'40" until 0'59". This tune consists of four musical phrases. Which of the following best describes the pattern of these four phrases? Ring your answer.

AAAA   ABAC   AABA   AABC

(d) Which of these rhythms matches the first repeated musical pattern that you hear in this extract? Ring your answer.

A   B
C   D

4. Listen to *Sahotas Boliyan* by the Sahotas THREE times before answering the following questions:

Sahotas Boliyan is available on *Bhangra Beatz* (Naxos World, 76012-2).

(a) Describe the music in the introduction to this track.

....

....

(b) (i) What other style of music is mixed with bhangra in this track? Ring your answer.

Jazz   Rap   Reggae   Salsa

(ii) Give one musical reason to support your answer.

....

(c) A synthesised string melody is played against the main vocal tune (eg at 0'39"). Ring the word that best describes the type of scale that this countermelody is based on.

Chromatic   Major   Minor   Whole-tone

(d) This track features traditional bhangra folk tunes. Briefly describe the sort of occasion when these folk tunes would have originally been performed.

....

Minimalism

5. Listen to the second movement of *New York Counterpoint* by Steve Reich THREE times before answering the following questions:

New York Counterpoint is available on *Minimalist Tendencies*, Clarinet Classics, CC00 24.

(a) What is the main instrument heard in this piece?

....

(b) What happens at the start?

☐ one instrument playing a solo

☐ two instruments playing the same melody in harmony

☐ two instruments playing the same melody in octaves

☐ two instruments playing the same melody in unison

(c) What minimalist techniques are used in this music?

....

(d) About half way through the piece (1'14" on the listed recording) a new musical idea is heard. Describe this new feature.

....

....

....

Traditions and Innovation

(e) This piece is performed entirely by one player. Describe how what you can hear might have been achieved.

....

....

....

6. Listen to *Short Ride in a Fast Machine* by John Adams THREE times before answering the following questions:

Short Ride in a Fast Machine is available on EMI Classics, CDC 5550512.

(a) (i) What percussion instrument do you hear at the very start of this piece?

....

(ii) Describe what this instrument does throughout the piece.

....

(b) Name three other percussion instruments that you hear in this piece.

....

(c) Describe the brass parts at the start of this piece.

....

....

(d) Suggest three ways in which the music reflects the title.

....

....

....

Glossary

Remember that you are expected to use technical terms correctly and you should be able to identify something when you hear it.

Accent. A special emphasis given to certain notes, usually by performing them louder than their surrounding notes.

Alto. A very high male or low female voice.

Amplification. The process of increasing the strength of an electrical signal.

Anacrusis. One or more notes preceding the first strong beat of a musical phrase.

Answering phrase. See **question and answer**.

Arco. A direction for string players to bow the strings, as opposed to plucking them (see **pizzicato**).

Arpeggio. A chord played as a series of single pitches in order from the lowest to the highest or vice-versa.

Articulation. 1. The point at which a note is sounded. **2.** The length of notes in relation to their context (eg legato as opposed to staccato articulation).

Atonal music. Music that is unrelated to a tonic note and so has no sense of key.

Balanced phrasing. Phrases of the same length paired together so that the first sounds like a question that is answered by the second phrase.

Baritone. A high bass voice.

Baroque music. Music typical of the period from about 1600–1750.

Bass. 1. A low male voice. **2.** The lowest-sounding part of a composition whether for voices or instruments.

Bhangra. A fusion of western pop styles and traditional Punjabi styles of music.

Binary form. A musical structure in two sections (AB).

Bitonality. The use of two different keys at the same time.

Blue note. See **blues scale**.

Blues scale. A scale in which some pitches (blue notes) are performed flatter than their counterparts in a major scale. The most commonly altered pitches are the third and seven degrees.

Bridge. 1. A linking passage between two important sections of a composition.

Cadence. A point of repose at the end of a phrase, sometimes harmonised with two cadence chords. See **imperfect cadence**, **interrupted cadence**, **perfect cadence** and **plagal cadence**.

Call and response. A type of music in which a soloist sings or plays a phrase to which a larger group responds with an answering phrase.

Chaal rhythm. Basic rhythm found in bhangra.

Chamber music. Music intended for domestic performance with one instrument per part.

Chóro. The group of singers in *son*/salsa.

Choir. A group of singers performing together, whether in unison or in parts.

Chorus. 1. In popular music, a setting of the refrain of the lyrics. **2.** A large group of singers usually performing in several parts. **3.** The electronic multiplication of a sound to give it greater body.

Chromatic notes. See **diatonic and chromatic notes**.

Chromatic scale. A scale of semitones that includes all 12 pitches commonly used in western music.

Classical music. 1. Art music of any period or country as opposed to folk music, jazz or pop. **2.** European art music, or music in European art-music styles, written in the second half of the 18th century and early 19th century.

Clave rhythm. In salsa, the central rhythmic pattern underlying the entire structure of the music, around which the other parts must fit. The rhythm is usually played on a pair of wooden sticks called claves.

Cluster chord. A chord made up of several pitches a step apart.

Coda. The final section of a movement or piece.

Compass. The range of an instrument from lowest to highest possible note.

Comping. In jazz, the rhythmic playing of chords to provide an accompaniment.

Compound time. See **simple and compound time**.

Concerto. A composition for one or more solo instruments accompanied by an orchestra.

Concord and discord. See **consonance and dissonance**.

Consonance and dissonance. The relative stability (consonance) or instability (dissonance) of two or more notes sounded simultaneously. Consonant intervals and chords are called concords. Dissonant intervals and chords are called discords.

Consort. In 16th- and 17th-century music an ensemble of instruments from the same family.

Continuo. 1. An abbreviation of basso continuo, a bass part in baroque music intended to be played on one or more bass instruments together with improvised chords above it and played on a harmony instrument. **2.** The group of two or more instrumentalists providing an accompaniment derived from the continuo bass part.

Contralto. A low female voice.

Contrapuntal. Adjective from counterpoint.

Countermelody. A new melody that occurs simultaneously with a melody that has been heard before.

Counterpoint. The simultaneous combination of two or more melodic lines. See also **polyphony**.

Cover version. An arrangement of a song performed by different musicians from those in the original recording.

Cross-rhythm. A rhythm that conflicts with the regular pattern of stressed and unstressed beats of a composition, or the combination of two conflicting rhythms within a single beat (eg duplets against triplets).

Crumhorn. A renaissance reed instrument shaped like a small hockey stick.

Cyclic. Often used to describe music based on the constant (and sometimes varied) repetition of a short phrase.

Da capo. An instruction to repeat from the beginning.

Decoration. Printed embellishments or departures from the written score intended to enrich a performance and provide variety in repeated passages.

Delay. An electronic effect which produces a copy of the input sound signal that lags behind the input by a specified amount of time.

Descant. A decorative line sung above the main melody of a hymn or similar vocal piece.

Development. The elaboration of previously-heard music by such means as modulation, sequences and inversion.

Dhol. A large cylindrical south-Asian drum, often used in bhangra.

Diatonic and chromatic notes. Diatonic notes are those belonging to the scale of the prevailing key while chromatic notes are foreign to it. For example in C major G is a diatonic note whereas G♯ is a chromatic note.

Discord. See **consonance and dissonance**.

Dissonance. See **consonance and dissonance**.

Divisions. A type of variation form in which the long notes of the theme are divided into shorter note values by the addition of extra notes.

Dominant. The fifth degree of a major or minor scale (eg D is the dominant in G major).

Dominant pedal. The fifth degree of a scale held or repeated against changing harmony.

Double stopping. The performance of a two-note chord on a bowed string instrument.

Doubling. The simultaneous performance of the same melody by two players or groups of players, either at the same pitch or in octaves.

Drone. The same as pedal, but the term is usually associated with folk music. A two-note drone usually consists of the tonic and dominant.

Drum machine. A synthesiser capable of simulating the sounds of a number of percussion instruments.

Dynamics. The loudness (f) and quietness (p) of notes.

Echo. The effect of a delay long enough to produce a distinct copy of a sound.

Episode. A distinct section within a movement.

Falsetto. A special vocal technique that enables a man to extend his range to higher pitches than usual.

Fanfare. A loud call to attention usually played on brass instruments and often with only the pitches of one or two simple chords.

Fermata. A sign (𝄐) that indicates a pause in the music.

Figure. Another name for a motif.

Flat. 1. A sign (♭) that lowers the pitch of a note by a semitone. One or more flat signs at the beginning of a stave make a key signature. Each flat in a key signature lowers notes with the same letter name by a semitone throughout the rest of the stave unless contradicted by an accidental or change in key signature. A flat inserted immediately in front of a note is an accidental and its effect only lasts until the end of the bar. **2.** An adjective describing a note that is sung or played at a lower pitch than it should be.

Fusion. Music in which two or more distinct styles are blended together, for example folk-rock.

FX. Pronounced 'effects', this term refers to various electronic ways to process sound, such as chorus, distortion, echo, reverb etc. The term is also used for pre-recorded sound effects used in film and broadcasting, such as the sound of rain falling.

Gavotte. A 17th and early 18th century dance in moderate $\frac{2}{2}$ time with phrases beginning with two crotchets on the second minim beat of the bar.

Genre. A category or group such as the piano sonata.

Gigue. The last movement of many baroque dance suites, the gigue is in fast compound time and often has regular four-bar phrases.

Glissando. A slide from one pitch to another.

Grace notes. Melodic ornaments indicated by small type.

Harmonic. A high-pitched pure sound produced by lightly touching the string of a violin, viola, cello, or double bass at a specific point while bowing it.

Harmonic progression. A series of chords.

Harmonic rhythm. A rhythmic pattern made by chord changes. Harmonic rhythm is often different from the rhythm of the melody.

Harmonic sequence. The immediate repetition of a progression of chords at a higher or lower pitch level.

Harmony. The combination of sounds to produce a chord or a progression of chords.

Harmony note. A note belonging to the current chord.

Heterophony. A texture made up of a simple tune and a more elaborate version of it played or sung together.

Homophony. A homophonic texture is one in which one part has all the melodic interest, while the other parts provide a simple accompaniment of chords or broken chords.

Hook. A short and memorable melodic or rhythmic idea in pop music.

Interlude. Music played between sections of a large work.

Imitation. A contrapuntal device in which a melodic idea stated in one part is copied in another part while the melodic line of the first part continues. Only the opening notes of the original melody need be repeated for this effect to be heard.

Imperfect cadence. An approach chord followed by chord V at the end of a phrase.

Improvisation. The creation or realisation of music while performing it.

Interrupted cadence. Chord V followed by an unexpected chord (such as VI) at the end of a phrase.

Interval. The distance between two pitches including both of the pitches that form the interval. So, in the scale of C major, the interval between the first and second notes is a 2nd (C–D), the interval between the second and fourth notes is a 3rd (D–E–F), and so on.

Introduction. A preparatory section before the main body of a composition.

Inversion. 1. The process of turning a melody upside down so that every interval of the original is kept but they all move in the opposite direction. **2.** A chord is inverted when a note other than the root is sounded in the bass. **3.** An interval is inverted when one of the two notes moves an octave so that instead of being below the second note it is above it (and vice versa).

Key. The relationship between the pitches of notes in music in which one particular pitch is more important than other pitches. This important note is called the tonic and its pitch determines the key of the music. So a composition in which C is the tonic is said to be 'in the key of C'.

Key signature. One or more flat signs (♭) or sharp signs (♯) placed immediately after a clef or double barline on a stave. The effect of each flat or sharp sign lasts throughout the stave and applies to all notes with the same letter name unless contradicted by accidentals or a change in key signature. A key signature usually gives some indication of the key of the music that follows it.

Layering. The process of building a piece of music by combining separate layers of sound. See also **multitracking** and **overdubbing**.

Leadsheet. Abbreviated method of writing a song or piece, giving words, melody, chord symbols and structure.

Leap. An interval of a 3rd or more between consecutive notes of a melody.

Legato. A smooth performance of music without any breaks between successive notes.

Loop. See **tape loop**.

Lute. A fretted plucked string instrument popular in the renaissance and baroque periods, used for solo performance and accompaniment.

Lyrics. The text of a song.

Major and minor. A major interval is greater than a minor interval by a semitone. The interval between the first and third degrees of a major scale is four semitones, one semitone greater than the interval between the same degrees in a minor scale.

Melisma. A group of notes sung to one syllable.

Melodic inversion. See **inversion 1**.

Melodic sequence. The immediate repetition of a melodic fragment in the same part at a different pitch level. There is a melodic sequence in the British national anthem at the words 'Send her victorious/Happy and glorious'.

Melody and accompaniment. The melody is the line of a piece of music where choice and arrangement of pitch, duration and intervals are intended to provide primary interest. It is often played on higher instruments, for example violin, flute, trumpet (and piano right hand). The accompaniment is the part of the music which supports the melody and tends to be written on deeper-sounding instruments, eg trombone, double bass (and piano left hand).

Metre. The organisation of the beat into repeating patterns of strong and weak pulses.

Metronome mark. A symbol for a note value, an equals sign and a number at the beginning of a composition. The note value is the beat and the number shows how many beats there should be per minute. Thus ♩ = 60 means there should be 60 crotchet beats per minute.

Microtone. An interval smaller than a semitone.

Middle eight. The third phrase in the chorus of 32-bar popular song song form (AABA – the middle eight is B). Like the other three phrases it is often eight bars long. Also called the bridge.

MIDI. Musical Instrument Digital Interface: a system for exchanging music performance data between suitably equipped computers and/or instruments.

Minuet, minuetto. An elegant dance in $\frac{3}{4}$ which was the only dance of the baroque period to be retained in classical instrumental music where it formed a ternary movement with a trio (minuet–trio–minuet).

Mixing desk. A device for processing, combining and monitoring audio signals, usually with a view to producing a final two-channel (stereo) output.

Modal music. Music based on one of the scales of seven pitch classes commonly found in western music, but excluding the major and minor scales.

Modulation. The harmonic or melodic process by which music moves from one key to another.

Monophony. A single unaccompanied melody, whether for a soloist or for unison voices or instruments.

Montuno. A section in *son* and salsa where the lead singers or instrumentalists improvise.

Motif. A short melodic or rhythmic idea that is sufficiently distinctive to allow it to be modified, manipulated and possibly combined with other motifs while retaining its own identity. Also spelled motive.

Multitracking. A recording technique where several tracks of sound are recorded independently but are played back together.

Mute. A device fitted to an instrument to dampen the sound.

Natural. A sign (♮) that cancels the effect of one of the symbols in a key signature, or cancels the effect of a previous accidental.

Note clusters. See **cluster chord**.

Octave. The interval between any note and the pitch of the next note above or below it with the same letter name. The two notes that form an octave are 12 semitones apart.

On-beat and off-beat notes. Notes articulated on the beat and off the beat respectively.

Opera. A dramatic fusion of words, music, spectacle and sometimes dancing.

Ornamentation. Decorative notes that flesh out a melodic skeleton. There are hundreds of types of ornament. They can be printed in ordinary type, printed as small grace notes, indicated by conventional symbols or added by the performer.

Ostinato. A rhythmic, melodic or harmonic pattern played many times in succession. See also **riff**.

Overdubbing. The process of adding a new musical part to a recording in synchronisation with previously recorded tracks.

Overture. An instrumental prelude to a large work such as an opera or oratorio. The term is sometimes used as the title for an independent orchestral work in one movement.

Pan. The electronic placing of a sound source at a particular position (from far left to far right) in a stereo soundfield.

Passing note. A decorative melody note filling the gap between two harmony notes.

Pedal. A sustained or repeated note sounded against changing harmony.

Pentatonic music. Music based on a scale of five different pitches.

Perfect cadence. Chords V and I at the end of a phrase.

Phasing. A gently undulating delay effect in which the delay-time is gradually changed.

Phrase. Part of a melody which requires the addition of another phrase or phrases to make complete musical sense.

Phrasing. The way a melody divides up into shorter sections called phrases, and the way a performer makes the phrases clear by an appropriate use of legato and staccato, dynamic changes and other nuances.

Pipe. An end-blown flute a bit like a recorder.

Pitch. The height or depth of a note. This can be expressed in relatively vague terms ('the pitch of that note is A', or even 'that is a high-pitched note'), or it can be expressed in absolute terms ('the pitch of this A is 440 vibrations per second').

Pitch names. The letters from A to G which are used to identify the pitches of notes on a stave.

Pizzicato. A direction to string players to pluck rather then bow the strings.

Plagal cadence. Chords IV and I at the end of a phrase.

Plainchant. Monophonic sacred music.

Polyphony. As used most frequently today polyphony means the same as counterpoint – a texture made up of two or more melodies sounding together.

Polyrhythm. The simultaneous combination of two or more distinctly different and often conflicting types of rhythm.

Portamento. A slide from one pitch to another.

Prelude. An introductory movement such as the overture to an opera. In the 19th and 20th centuries this term was used as a title for an independent instrumental piece in any form or style.

Primary triads. Chords I, IV and V.

Progression. The movement from one note to another in

a melody, or from one chord to another in harmony. See **harmonic progression**.

Pulse. Beat.

Quantise. The process of automatically adjusting data on sequencers to fit within defined limits.

Question and answer. A term for two phrases, the first of which seems to pose a question (and so ends with an inconclusive cadence such as I–V) followed by a similar phrase that seems to provide the answer (and so ends with a conclusive cadence such as V–I).

Rāg (raga). A pattern of ascending and descending notes associated with particular moods and used as the basis for melodic improvisation in Indian classical music.

Range. The distance between the lowest and highest notes of a melody or composition, or the distance between the highest and lowest notes that can be played on an instrument or sung by a particular type of voice.

Reel. A dance in fast $\frac{2}{4}$ time popular in the British Isles, Scandinavia and America.

Refrain. A repeated passage of music and/or words, such as the chorus of a pop song.

Register. A part of the range of a voice or instrument. The lowest pitches of a clarinet form the chalumeau register.

Relative major and relative minor. Two keys that share the same key signature but whose tonic notes are a minor 3rd apart, such as G major and E minor.

Remix. In popular music, translating a work into a different style using electronic manipulation.

Repetition. In music, the restatement of a passage that has already been performed.

Retrograde. Backwards. For instance, the notes A–B–C–D become D–C–B–A in retrograde order.

Reverb. An abbreviation of reverberation, the prolonging of a sound caused by its complex reflections between the walls, floor and ceiling of a room or hall. The effect can be created electronically and applied to music (including acoustic music picked up by a microphone).

Rhythmic counterpoint. Two or more clearly defined and independent rhythms played simultaneously.

Riff. In jazz or pop, a short, memorable melodic pattern repeated many times in succession. See also **ostinato**.

Romantic music. Music in which the emotional message is at least as important as the form in which it is expressed. Romantic music can be found throughout the history of western music, but it was particularly obvious in most of the music composed between about 1820 and 1914.

Rondo. A composition in which a passage of music heard at the start is repeated several times, the repeats being separated from each other by contrasting passages of music known as episodes.

Root. In tonal music, the fundamental pitch of any chord built from superimposed 3rds. The fundamental pitch of a dominant triad (chord V) is the fifth degree of the scale of the prevailing key. If the key is C major the root of chord V is G, no matter which of the three pitches of chord V (G, B and D) is the bass note.

Rubato. 'Robbed time'. Expressive changes to the position of beats within a bar, sometimes leading to expressive fluctuations in the overall tempo (common in some types of romantic music).

Salsa. Latin-American dance style influenced by *son* and jazz.

Sampler. A device for recording sections of sounds (samples) as digital information. It allows them to be played back with various modifications (eg at different speeds, in continuous loops or in combination with other samples).

Sarabande. A slow dance in triple time found in many baroque suites.

Scale. A collection of pitches that can be derived from a piece of music and arranged in stepwise ascending and descending order.

Scalic. An adjective referring to a melodic contour in which adjacent notes move by step in a similar manner to notes in a scale.

Semitone. The interval between two adjacent pitches on a keyboard instrument (including black notes). It is the smallest interval in common use in western music.

Sequence. The immediate repetition of a motif or phrase of a melody in the same part but at a different pitch. A harmonic progression can be treated in the same way. The repetition may be at a higher pitch (creating an ascending sequence) or at a lower pitch (creating a descending sequence).

Sequencer. Computer software (or more rarely a purpose-built electronic device) for the input, editing and playback of music performance data using MIDI.

Serial music. Music based on manipulations of a series of 12 notes including every pitch of the chromatic scale.

Setting. Music added to a text so that the words are sung instead of spoken.

Seventh chord. A triad plus a note a 7th above the root. The dominant 7th consists of a major triad on the fifth degree of the scale (eg G–B–D in C major) plus a minor 7th above the root (F). In the same key a tonic 7th consists of a major triad on the first degree of the scale (C–E–G) plus a major 7th above the root (B).

Sharp. 1. A sign (♯) which raises the pitch of a note by a semitone. One or more sharp signs at the beginning of a stave make a key signature. Each sharp in a key signature raises notes with the same letter by a semitone throughout the rest of the stave unless contradicted by an accidental or change in key signature. A sharp inserted immediately in front of a note is an accidental and its effect only lasts until the end of the bar. **2.** An adjective describing a note that is sung or played at a higher pitch than it should be.

Silence. An absence of intentional sound.

Simple and compound time. In simple time the beat is usually a minim (eg $\frac{2}{2}$ and $\frac{3}{2}$) or a crotchet (eg $\frac{2}{4}$ and $\frac{3}{4}$). In both cases the beat can divide into two, four or eight shorter notes. In compound time the beat is usually a dotted minim (eg $\frac{6}{4}$) or dotted crotchet (eg $\frac{6}{8}$ and $\frac{9}{8}$). In both cases the beat can divide into three, six or 12 shorter notes.

Sitar. A north-Indian fretted plucked string instrument, with a number of melody strings, drone strings and sympathetic strings.

Solo. Music for a single performer, with or without accompaniment.

Son. Cuban dance style that influenced salsa.

Sonata. An instrumental composition, usually in several movements or sections, written for a single instrument or a small ensemble of instruments.

Soprano. A high female or unbroken boy's voice.

Staccato. Detached. An indication that notes are to be separated and not sustained for their full length.

Staff notation. A staff or stave consists of five horizontal lines. These and the spaces between them are assigned specific pitches by a treble ($\treble$), bass ($\bass$) or C clef ($\cclef$). Staff notation consists of a stave, a clef and notes printed on, between, above or below the lines of the stave.

Step. A semitone or tone, or one of the degrees of a scale.

Strophic. A song in which the same music is used for every stanza (verse) of the text.

Subdominant. The fourth degree of a major or minor scale (eg C in G major).

Subito (sub.). Immediately.

Suite. A collection of pieces intended to be performed together. In the baroque suite a number of dances in binary form and all in the same key were grouped together to form the dance suite. Later suites could consist of a series of extracts from an opera, ballet or musical.

Swing quavers, swung quavers. The division of the beat into pairs of notes in which the first is longer than the second. In music notation this ♩♪ approximates to the pattern.

Symphony. A large-scale composition for orchestra, usually in four movements.

Syncopation. Accentuation of notes sounded off the beat or on a weak beak, often with rests or the second of a pair of tied notes on some of the strong beats.

Synthesiser. An electronic instrument that can produce and modify sound. It can be used to imitate other musical instruments and to produce non-musical sounds.

Tabla. A pair of Indian drums played with hands and fingers by a single performer.

Tabor. A small drum.

Tāl (tala). A cyclic pattern in Indian music that forms the basis for rhythmic improvisation.

Tanpura. An instrument similar in shape to the sitar, but with a smaller sound-box and a longer neck. The instrument has four strings which are used to play a drone.

Tape loop. A section of magnetic tape fixed end to end so that the same music can be repeated indefinitely. The process is now usually accomplished using digital technology.

Tempo. The speed of a composition, usually measured by the speed of the beat. This can be indicated by a tempo mark (eg *presto*), a metronome mark (eg ♩ = 120), or both.

Tenor. A high male voice.

Ternary form. A three-part structure (ABA) in which the first and last sections are identical or very similar. These enclose a contrasting central section.

Texture. The number and timbres of parts in a composition and the way they relate to each other.

Theme and variations. A composition in which a theme is repeated, each time with alterations to one or more of its original elements. The theme can be a melody, a bass ostinato, a progression of chords, or a combination of any or all of them.

Tie. A curved line joining the heads of two notes of the same pitch. It shows that the time values of the two notes should be added together to form one long note.

Timbre. The tone colour of an instrument or voice.

Time signature. Two numbers, one on top of the other. Usually the upper number indicates the number of beats per bar and the lower number indicates the time value of the beat. See **simple and compound time.**

Tonal music. Music based in a clearly defined key. A key is established by the relationships between the pitches of major and minor scales. The most important relationship is that between the tonic (the first degree of a scale) and all other pitches.

Tone. 1. An interval of two semitones, eg C–D. **2.** A sound of definite pitch. **3.** The timbre of a particular instrument or voice.

Tone row. A series of 12 different pitches used as the basis of a composition in serial music.

Tonic. The first degree of a major or minor scale.

Tonic pedal. The first degree of a scale held or repeated against changing harmony.

Transposition. The performance or notation of a passage of music or of a whole piece at a pitch-level higher or lower than the original.

Treble. An unbroken boy's voice.

Tremolo. The fast and continuous repetition of a single note.

Tres. A Cuban instrument with three pairs of strings. Modelled on the Spanish guitar.

Triad. A chord of three pitches consisting of a fundamental pitch called the root and notes pitched a 3rd and a 5th above it.

Trill. A melodic ornament consisting of the rapid alternation of two pitches a step apart.

Trio. 1. Music for three solo performers. **2.** Music for a single performer written throughout in three contrapuntal parts. **3.** The middle section of the minuet–trio–minuet group that forms the third movement of many classical symphonies and string quartets.

Triplet. A group of three notes of equal length intended to be played in the time of two notes of the same time-value.

Tritone. An interval of three tones, eg F–B.

Turn. A four-note ornament consisting of the note above the main note, the main note itself, the note below the main note and the main note once again.

Tutti. A passage in which all or most of the members of an ensemble are playing.

Twelve-bar blues. A structure that originated in blues songs which has been widely adopted in jazz and pop music. The melody, which usually includes blue notes, consists of three four-bar phrases, the second often being a repeat of the first. The chord structure is built around chords I, IV and V.

Unison. The combined sound of two or more notes of the same pitch.

Up-tempo. Fast, lively speed.

Variations. A musical structure in which a theme is repeated, each time with alterations to one or more of its original elements.

Verse. In a pop song, sections that contrast with the chorus.

Verse and chorus. A standard form used in popular song in which a chorus is repeated after most verses.

Viol. One of a family of bowed string instruments.

Virginals. A small harpsichord.

Virtuoso. A performer of outstanding technical brilliance.

Walking bass. A steady bass part usually in notes of the same time-value.

Waltz. A triple-time dance of the 19th and early 20th centuries with an on-beat accompaniment in which the lowest note is sounded on the first beat of the bar followed by upper notes of the chord on beats 2 and 3 (um-cha-cha). The tempo ranges from moderate to fast.

Whole-tone music. Music based on a scale that consists of whole-tone steps.

Tempo markings

The following are some of the most common tempo marks arranged alphabetically:

Accelerando (accel.)	Getting faster
Adagio	Slow
Allargando	Getting slower
Allegro	Fast
Andante	Moderately slow
Crescendo (cresc.)	Gradually getting louder
Diminuendo (dim.)	Gradually getting softer
Largo	Slow
Moderato	At a moderate tempo
Presto	Very fast
Rallentando (rall.)	Slowing down
Ritenuto (rit.)	Immediately slowing down
Vivace	Lively

Dynamic markings

The following are some of the most common dynamic markings arranged alphabetically:

Forte (f)	Loud
Fortissimo (ff)	Very loud
Mezzoforte (mf)	Moderately loud
Mezzopiano (mp)	Moderately soft
Pianissimo (pp)	Very quiet
Piano (p)	Quiet
Sforzando (sf, sfz)	Strongly accented